ENCYCLOPEDIA OF BRAZILIAN JIU-JITSU

VOLUME 3

by

RIGAN MACHADO

and

JOSE M. FRADUAS

LES YANOVER
(206) 910-9500

UP

UNIQUE PUBLICATIONS
Burbank, California

Disclaimer
Please note that the author and publisher of this book are not responsible in any manner whatsoever for any injury that may result from practicing the techniques and/or following the instructions given within. Because the physical activities described herein may be too strenuous in nature for some readers to engage in safely, it is essential that a physician be consulted prior to training.

First published in 2004 by Unique Publications.

Library of Congress Cataloging-in-Publication Data

Machado, Rigan.
Encyclopedia of Brazilian jiu jitsu / Rigan Machado and Jose M. Fraguas. 1st ed.
p. cm.
Includes index.
ISBN 0-86568-224-0 (pbk. : alk. paper) -- ISBN 0-86568-229-1
(pbk. : alk. paper) -- ISBN 0-86568-230-5 (pbk. : alk. paper)

1. Jiu-jitsu—Brazil—Encyclopedias. I. Fraguas, Jose M. II. Title.
GV1114.M339 2004
796.815 '2' 0898103—dc22

2004002550

Library of Congress Catalog Number: 2004002550
ISBN: 0-86568-230-5
Unique Publications
4201 Vanowen Place
Burbank, CA 91505
(800) 332-3330

First edition

Printed in the United States of America.

Editor: Doug Jeffrey
Design: Willy Blumhoff
Cover Design: George Chen

"Victories that are cheap are cheap.
Those only are worth having which come
as the result of hard fighting."

—Henry Ward Beecher

Dedication

To the memory of Carlos Gracie, the first member of the Gracie family who trained in the art of Jiu-Jitsu.

To Professor Helio Gracie, a true pioneer who broke barriers and put himself to test on behalf of his beloved art. His study and sacrifice paved the road for all future generations.

Acknowledgements

The creation of the *Encyclopedia of Brazilian Jiu-Jitsu* has been very much a team effort since the authors conceived this book in 2001.

Special thanks to the members of the Machado and Gracie family, whose permission to quote and peruse from personal notes has given this text its core.

To Doug Jeffrey, editor of the work, for his time and effort cleaning and polishing the manuscript. Your help and dedication are truly appreciated.

To Todd Hester, editor of *Grappling* magazine, for his encouragement and expert advice for this work.

To Carlos Gracie Jr., president of the Brazilian Confederation of Jiu-Jitsu from Rio de Janeiro, Brazil, for his priceless support and cooperation throughout the project.

Additional thanks are extended to Kid Peligro, a columnist of *Grappling* and *Gracie* magazines and dedicated Brazilian Jiu-Jitsu practitioner, who allowed the authors to use some photos from his personal archives.

To Jaimee Itagaki, photographer at CFW Enterprises, who put in many hours behind the camera capturing all the technical details.

To all the students who provided excellent cooperation and skills while demonstrating the techniques that you see on these pages.

Finally, we want to thank all the students and practitioners around the world whose support and dedication to the art has tremendously helped to promote and popularize the art of Brazilian Jiu-Jitsu.

Table of Contents

About the Authors

RIGAN MACHADO

Rigan Machado, whose lineage is linked directly to the art's founder, Carlos Gracie, is one of the top Brazilian Jiu-Jitsu instructors in the world. His long experience in teaching — to everyone from beginners to world champions — and his contributions to the art's teaching methods have brought him worldwide acclaim. Originally from Rio de Janeiro, Brazil, Machado's personal credits include many of the top Brazilian national and international championships. Furthermore, Rigan Machado was one of the first Brazilian black belts who moved from Brazil to the United States of America, where he became one of the leading forces in expanding the art. *"Brazil was just the beginning of the grappling movement,"* says Machado. *"From there, the seeds have been spread all around the world. If a student is not from Brazil and he becomes a world champion, then that makes me a good teacher and makes me happy."*

Despite his fame, he continues to train with a dedication born out of the love of his art. Machado has also appeared in several movies and television shows, becoming one of the most recognizable figures in the world of the martial arts. Highly regarded as one of the most talented technicians and teachers who ever came out of the Gracie family, Rigan has been instrumental in the development of Machado Jiu-Jitsu as it is known today.

"Finding a harmony between mind and body is the ultimate goal of any martial artist, but the physical techniques must come first," he says. *"A calm and concentrated awareness is the key toward the realization of personal potential, of which the technical mastery is the first step."*

Drawing from his considerable knowledge, Rigan Machado has written extensively on his art and authored several series of DVD's on Brazilian Jiu-Jitsu through Unique Publications.

JOSE M. FRAGUAS

Born on October 25, 1962, Jose M. Fraguas had his first contact with the martial arts (the grappling art of Judo) at the age of nine. Practicing as a child under Sensei Young Lee in Madrid, Spain, Fraguas progressed rapidly until he decided to pursue a different but related martial art style. The seeds of contact sports, however, had been planted.

Recognized as an international authority on the martial arts and author of many books on the subject, he began his career as a writer at age 16 by serving as a regular contributor to martial arts magazines in Great Britain, France, Spain, Italy, Germany, Portugal, Holland and Australia. Having hands-on experience and training allowed him to better reflect the physical side of the martial arts in his writing. He started his training in Brazilian Jiu-Jitsu in the late 1980s with several members of the Gracie family.

"I would love to mention the members of the Gracie family who spent so many hours in private and group classes sharing their knowledge with me, but I am afraid that crediting them with being responsible for my Jiu-Jitsu skills would make them feel more pain than pride," Fraguas says laughing.

His desire to promote both ancient philosophy and modern thinking provided the motivation for writing this book. *"I want to write books so I can learn as well as share."* Fraguas continues, *"The martial arts are like life itself. Both are filled with experiences that seem quite ordinary at the time and assume a fabled stature only with the passage of the years. I hope this work will be appreciated by future practitioners of the art of Brazilian Jiu-Jitsu."*

Currently living in Los Angeles, California, Fraguas is the General Manager of CFW Enterprises, the world's leading martial arts publishing company.

He can be contacted at: ***mastersseries@yahoo.com***

History

PART 3

"The problem was that the UFC was never meant to be safe for the fighters. Only two rules governed the event: no eye gouging and no biting. Everything else was allowed. It was as raw as it could get."

THE "ULTIMATE FIGHTING CHAMPIONSHIP"

In November 1993, the history of Brazilian Jiu-Jitsu reached a major turning point when Rorion Gracie, the eldest son of Helio Gracie, created the *Ultimate Fighting Championship*. The event was televised on pay-per-view and attracted the attention not only of all the martial artists in the world but also of politicians who tried to stop the event due to the lack of safety rules for the fighters. The problem was that the UFC was never meant to be safe for the fighters. Fighters were fighters and they were there to fight. Only two rules governed the event: no eye gouging and no biting. Everything else was allowed. It was as raw as it could get.

With a cage called the "Octagon" designed by famous film director and Jiu-Jitsu student John Milius, the UFC was meant to duplicate the Vale-Tudo (anything goes) no-hold-barred fights that the Gracie

family had done in Brazil for more than a half-century. It was meant to prove which techniques and fighting styles were truly efficient for one-on-one fighting. The limited rules allowed representatives of every style to use any technique they thought suitable. There were no weight classes, no time limits. It was as real as a sport could get and marked a dramatic turning point in the explosion of Brazilian Jiu-Jitsu around the world.

Royce Gracie, one of the younger sons of Helio Gracie, represented Brazilian Jiu-Jitsu in the UFC. The "Gracie Kid," as he was referred to by many at that time, ran over all his opponents in the first four UFCs. He displayed a calm strategy and submitted all his opponents using the techniques his father Helio had developed over the years. Martial artists and fighters from all over the world were shocked to see how the smaller and weaker Royce could not only control bigger and heavier opponents, but also choke them at will without getting hurt. He methodically closed the distance, got into a clinch, took his opponents to the ground and finished them with a clean choke or armbar.

The aftermath of the UFC took the popularity of Brazilian Jiu-Jitsu (or BJJ as it came to be known) to every corner of the world. Soon, countries such as Japan were offering great opportunities for other Jiu-Jitsu fighters to prove the efficiency of the art against skilled fighters. Rickson Gracie and Jean-Jacques Machado were two of the main proponents of the art who regularly visited Japan to fight. With the success of BJJ fighters, the demand for instructors became overwhelming and many Brazilian black belts decided to move to the U.S. to share their knowledge. Nothing would be the same in the world of martial arts as Brazilian Jiu-Jitsu suddenly reached every corner of the globe.

"Known for not holding back any knowledge of the art, Machado students soon became a leading force in BJJ and NHB competitions around the world."

MACHADO JIU-JITSU

One of the first groups of instructors to teach Brazilian Jiu-Jitsu internationally were the Machado brothers. Carlos, Rigan, Roger, John and Jean-Jacques, the sons of Luiza (the sister-in-law of Carlos Gracie), have been instrumental in developing and expanding the art within the U.S.

They began to practice at an early age and soon found themselves training alongside other members of the Gracie family, spending many hours perfecting their techniques at Helio's famous family ranch in Teresopolis. With their main headquarters now in California, their passion and dedication for sharing Jiu-Jitsu caused a great number of students to embrace the South American art. Known for not holding back any knowledge of the art, Machado students soon became a leading force in BJJ and NHB competitions around the world.

"The five brothers have made important additions to the art by incorporating elements from arts such as Wrestling and Sambo into their arsenal."

The Machado brothers understood that to have good students, time and effort had to be expended on their part. They unselfishly dedicated a great amount of their time to bring out the best in their students, instead of focusing on their own competition careers. They felt driven to give others the gift of Jiu-Jitsu that they had received. While Rigan, John, Roger and Jean-Jacques relocated to different areas in the state of California to better expand the art, Carlos Machado moved to Dallas, Texas, where he opened an academy and taught legendary karate champion and television and film star Chuck Norris, the star of *Walker: Texas Ranger*. Norris soon became a true believer of Brazilian Jiu-Jitsu and threw himself into learning it. He also helped to promote the art through his show by giving the

Machado brothers several guest appearances in many of the series episodes. The Machado brothers' reputation soon spread and other martial art movie stars such as Steven Seagal offered them guest appearances in their action films.

The friendly and easy-going attitude of the Machado brothers caused open-minded martial arts experts such as Dan Inosanto to study and learn under their tutelage. These various masters already had excellent reputations in their own styles, and the Machados took the opportunity to observe and absorb technical and tactical elements from other non-grappling fighting arts and incorporate them into the structure of Machado Jiu-Jitsu.

Although Machado Jiu-Jitsu is not a new method or different style of Brazilian Jiu-Jitsu, the five brothers have made important additions to the art by incorporating elements from arts such as Wrestling and Sambo into their arsenal. They incorporated useful material and blended it into the strong technical structure they already possessed. This approach soon proved itself in trials by fire when Rigan and Jean-Jacques entered the *Abu Dhabi Combat Club* tournament in the United Arab Emirates with excellent results, beating some of the top grappling stylists from around the world, including world Judo, Wrestling and Sambo experts. In 1999, Jean-Jacques gave the greatest grappling performance ever witnessed when he won all his matches by submission and was awarded the title, "Most Technical Grappler in the World."

"With open minds, the Machados researched, grew, and expanded the art of Brazilian Jiu-Jitsu in every technical area."

But the true benefit of their methods have been proven by their students who have become national champions and won many important sport Jiu-Jitsu championships around the world. With open minds that allowed them to research, grow, and expand the art of Brazilian Jiu-Jitsu in every technical area, the Machado brothers have become the most sought-after Brazilian Jiu-Jitsu instructors anywhere. They are a leading force in its growth, not only in the United States, but also around the world.

THE YARD
HOWARD
HOWAR
COMBAT KIMON
HOWARD
COMBAT KIMONOS

Introduction

CHOOSING AN INSTRUCTOR

Being able to perform all Jiu-Jitsu techniques won't make you an instructor in the art. Doing and teaching are two completely different things and as such should be understood separately. As a student, you should be able to perform the physical techniques with a skill level accorded your rank. As an instructor, the physical ability won't make your students good Jiu-Jitsu practitioners. It is the ability to communicate, break down and pass the technical knowledge that is important here. Many great champions, in all kinds of sports, lacked the ability to break down everything they were capable of doing and teach it to their students. They were talented athletes but with no ability to create other talented athletes or good students.

Teaching Brazilian Jiu-Jitsu requires an extensive knowledge of how all the pieces of the puzzle (techniques) fit and the fundamental principles that every single technique exemplifies. A good teacher will have a progressive program that will allow the student not only to physically improve, but also understand how the different techniques are interrelated and how those can be combined in a practical format.

"Many great champions, in all kinds of sports, lacked the ability to break down everything they were capable of doing, and teach it to their students."

Although it is very common to see an instructor giving techniques in a random manner, this approach is definitely not the most appropriate for students to understand what they are doing. An instructor should start showing the student the basics of the art. The basic techniques develop the most fundamental principles found in the art. Most importantly, this is teaching the student the necessary body mechanics for future technical growth. Like any other martial art system, Brazilian Jiu-Jitsu has a set of fundamental techniques that a good instructor should emphasize in the early stages of learning. These basic techniques should be backed up with several drills — not fighting drills — that improve the student's ability to move his body on the ground. The drills eventually will make it possible to perform the technique properly.

"An experienced instructor will teach an armlock differently to a white belt, a purple belt and a black belt, depending on their expertise and knowledge of the art."

Beware of instructors who show too many techniques in a random way without giving a strong foundation to the student. Be cautious of those teachers who allow beginners to spar almost immediately — focusing on a competition approach and how the techniques are supposed to be used in a tournament — and force them to struggle in a grappling situation without previous intensive training and understanding of the basics. These types of instructors will push the student to perform the technique via pure strength and muscle, but this will eventually cut the student's progress in the art since all the basic information added to the database has been wrong. It is easier for these kinds of instructors to have students spar than to dedicate time to correct and teach the art properly. There is a time for everything and sparring in Brazilian Jiu-Jitsu should be incorporated into the student's program at the right time.

A good instructor will get any student — regardless of level of understanding and physical ability — to learn and apply a basic movement. It is up to the instructor to be able of dissect the technique and communicate the intrinsic principles of the movement to different levels of understanding. An experienced instructor will teach an armlock differently to a white belt, a purple belt and a black belt, depending on their expertise and knowledge of the art. It is the ability of the instructor to break down the information according to the student's level (technical and understanding) that sets a master apart from an average instructor. There are no bad students; only teachers incapable of making the student good at Jiu-Jitsu.

Find a teacher who dedicates time and attention to explaining the art and the techniques properly; someone who has a teaching structure and the correct methodology. No art or subject of any kind can be properly taught without a correct structure and format.

Finally, when looking for a Jiu-Jitsu instructor, simply remember that the students are a reflection of what the teacher is. Pay attention to the students, analyze how they train, how they move, and how they behave with lower ranks, such as explaining the techniques. See if they "compete" with the lower ranks or help them to improve. If you are planning to join a school and find that all the students do is "roll" indiscriminately, fight with no sense of technique or finesse and focus excessively on competing, maybe you need to keep looking.

TOURNAMENTS AND COMPETITION

Tournaments are an important part of most martial arts styles, but when practicing a martial art you must take into consideration what the real goal of the art is because ultimately a martial art is something different than a sport. Rules in competition, in any kind of competition, set the direction in which the physical techniques of the art/sport will evolve.

The ultimate goal of Jiu-Jitsu is to control and submit your opponent. Only these aspects represent the true superiority of one fighter over another. The problem arises when two excellent competitors meet and the "ideal" submission technique is blocked and countered by the other fighter. This situation provokes both participants to try to stall and play with the rules — using excessive force to get out of a position in which the opponent gets more points even if the fighter is not truly in any danger.

Jiu-Jitsu competition rules vary and change according to the specific tournament and those running it, but the essence of our Jiu-Jitsu training — when practiced at the school — shouldn't be governed by the set rules of the sport. Training in the art of Jiu-Jitsu and being good at it should be our main concern, not simply winning tournaments. Jiu-Jitsu is first and foremost a martial art and a sport second. When you step onto the mat and you are rolling with your partners, you try to do your best, regardless of how many points are awarded in competition for any specific movement.

"The ultimate goal of Jiu-Jitsu is to control and submit your opponent. Only these aspects represent the true superiority of one fighter over another."

Develop your game plan based on the concept and principles of a martial art, and later on, if you feel interested in competition, learn the rules and try to use them appropriately without forgetting that trying to control and submit your opponent is the main objective of Brazilian Jiu-Jitsu. In a perfect world, referees should only award points for either controlling the opponent clearly and with a full controlled technique for a certain amount of time (several seconds) or for putting the opponent into a submission and making him tap. This way, the competitors should have to train to fully control and totally submit their opponents.

Once you get into a tournament, make sure you know the rules and how to play with the regulations to get the best out of them. There is nothing wrong with using the rules of competition to your advantage. However, always keep in mind that sport competition has limits and regulations that don't measure your self-defense abilities, your personal involvement or the totality of your skill in the art.

In competition, the participants are grouped into similar levels of rank and skill. Therefore, as much as possible, it is a match against theoretical equals. As a result, the key element in sport Jiu-Jitsu lies in other surrounding aspects of the technical training. Physical conditioning, strength training, power training, cardiovascular training and psychological make-up are the key attributes that will make a difference in the end.

"Attributes without refined technique are useless. It is important to bring the building blocks in the proper order to establish a strong foundation."

The best illustration is the iceberg analogy. The tip of the iceberg, the fraction that shows, represents the physical techniques of the art — the basic movements. All the rest, the physical attributes necessary to make that "tip" work in a fight, comprise the 90 percent that is below the ice. They are underwater, where you can't see them...but that certainly doesn't mean they don't exist.

Every martial arts system requires certain physical attributes from the practitioner to be able to fully apply the individual techniques of the art. Standing fighting arts require specific attributes such as timing, mobility, reflexes, eye-hand/foot coordination, etc. Grappling arts like Brazilian Jiu-Jitsu rely mostly on physical sensitivity, body positioning, isometric muscular strength, limberness, etc.

Since the "perfect" execution of a single technique depends on the practitioner's level of attribute development, it is important for the students to allocate time to develop these necessary attributes for their chosen arts. Analyze the attributes that specifically apply to Brazilian Jiu-Jitsu and work on them hard. By doing this, you'll improve the effectiveness of your technique. Do the attribute training once you have already developed a high technical level. Attributes without refined technique is useless. It is important to bring the building blocks in the proper order to establish a strong foundation. Technique first... everything else follows.

Today's competitors are more knowledgeable about all the technical possibilities available at arm's reach.

Hopefully, the knowledge of an additional technique may surprise your opponent and allow you to score a decisive point or completely submit your opponent, but with all the technical advancements, an exclusively technique approach simply is not sufficient. The competitor needs to be an athlete if he wants to become a Brazilian Jiu-Jitsu champion. The physical techniques now have to be supported by other "supplementary aspects" of fighting because the game has improved tremendously in the last decade.

The hours you spent on the mat are called "flight time." Leave the ego at the door and don't try to fight your partners. The school is not a competition or tournament, and it is not a fight; it is the place where you learn the art. If your partner doesn't cooperate, then ask him to slow down and make him understand that both of you are helping each other. Anybody with enough muscle power can fight and force his way through a technique. Doing it with refined technique and skill is reserved to the few who excel.

One good way of training intelligently is to roll with your opponent when no submissions are allowed. Neither you nor your opponent can go for a submission, armlock, choke or leglock. This takes the pressure out of trying to submit the training partner and allows the practitioner to smoothly roll with the opponent, which will eventually develop many of the important attributes in sparring or competition. In this specific training drill, there is no destination or submission so we can enjoy the journey more consciously and improve one of the most difficult aspects of the art of Brazilian Jiu-Jitsu — flow with your opponent.

"Start working hard on the basics, and work on the small details that make the technique work; leave the brute force at home and think of finesse instead of strength."

Finally, set a progressive training plan that allows you to get better and improve your game. Start working hard on the basics; work on the small details that make the technique work. Leave the brute force at home and think of finesse instead of strength. Try to discover how all the positions you are learning interrelate to each other, how you can move from a defensive movement into an attack, how to reverse an armlock and end up submitting your opponent with a choke, or how to escape from a headlock and finish your opponent with a leglock. All techniques are interchangeable, and you'll be surprised how the most advanced technique can be countered with a basic movement. Most of the time the solution to a big problem lies in a simple answer.

Takedowns And Throws

Vol. 3

Rigan adopts the orthodox right-handed sleeve and lapel grip (1). He moves closer to his opponent, releases the collar and grabs the waist (2). Next, Rigan releases the sleeve and grabs the opponent's right leg (3). He pulls up on the leg (4), creating space to begin his sweep (5-6).

Ultimately, his opponent ends up on the ground (7).

Rigan uses the orthodox right-handed sleeve and lapel grip (1). Rigan steps forward with his right foot, which creates pressure on his opponent (2). He then steps forward with his left foot (3) to prepare the inside sweep (4). This unbalances his opponent (5).

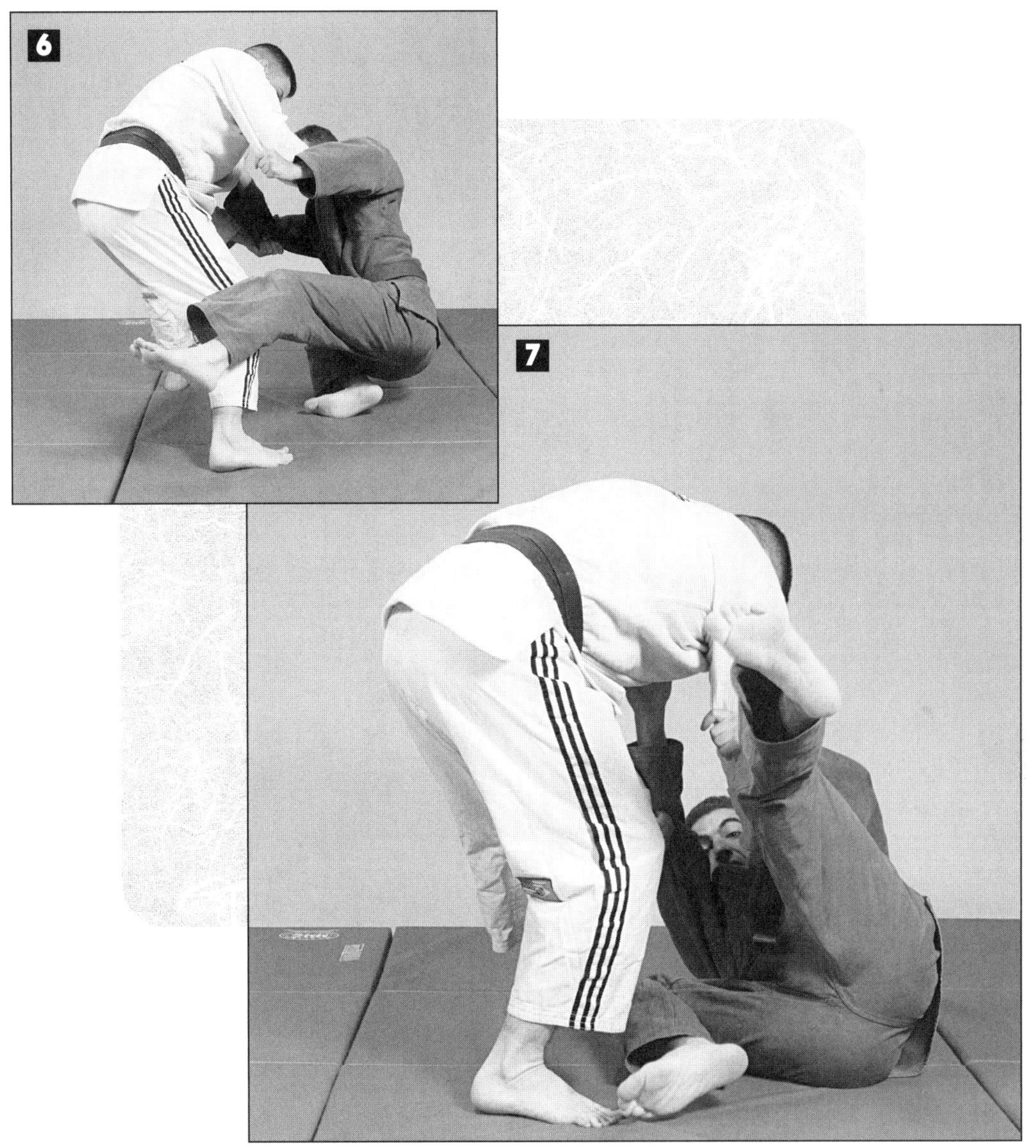

The adversary ends up on the floor (6-7).

Note: It is important to time the action of the leg with the pushing and control of the opponent's arms. The idea is to create a push/pull action.

Rigan employs the orthodox right-handed sleeve and lapel grip (1). To create pressure and prepare for the inside sweep, Rigan steps forward with his right foot (2) and then his left (3). Notice that he comes even closer than in the previous technique. To grab his opponent's left leg, he puts his right knee down (4-5).

This facilitates the takedown (6).

Rigan utilizes the orthodox right-handed sleeve and lapel grip (1). To create pressure, he steps in with his right foot (2). He immediately brings his left foot forward (3) to prepare the inside sweep (4).

This time the opponent feels the entry action and lifts his left leg (5), avoiding the sweep (6).

continued

continued from page 9

Rigan shifts his right foot forward (7) and begins to move his hips to the left (8) so he can control his opponent (9) and throw him.

11

12

13

Rigan throws his opponent over his right shoulder (10-12). He controls the opponent's right arm during the action so he gets better positioning for a follow-up technique (13).

Note: Bring your center of gravity down when giving your back to the opponent. By pulling with your arm and keeping your hips low, he will be unbalanced. This will make it impossible for him to prevent the throw.

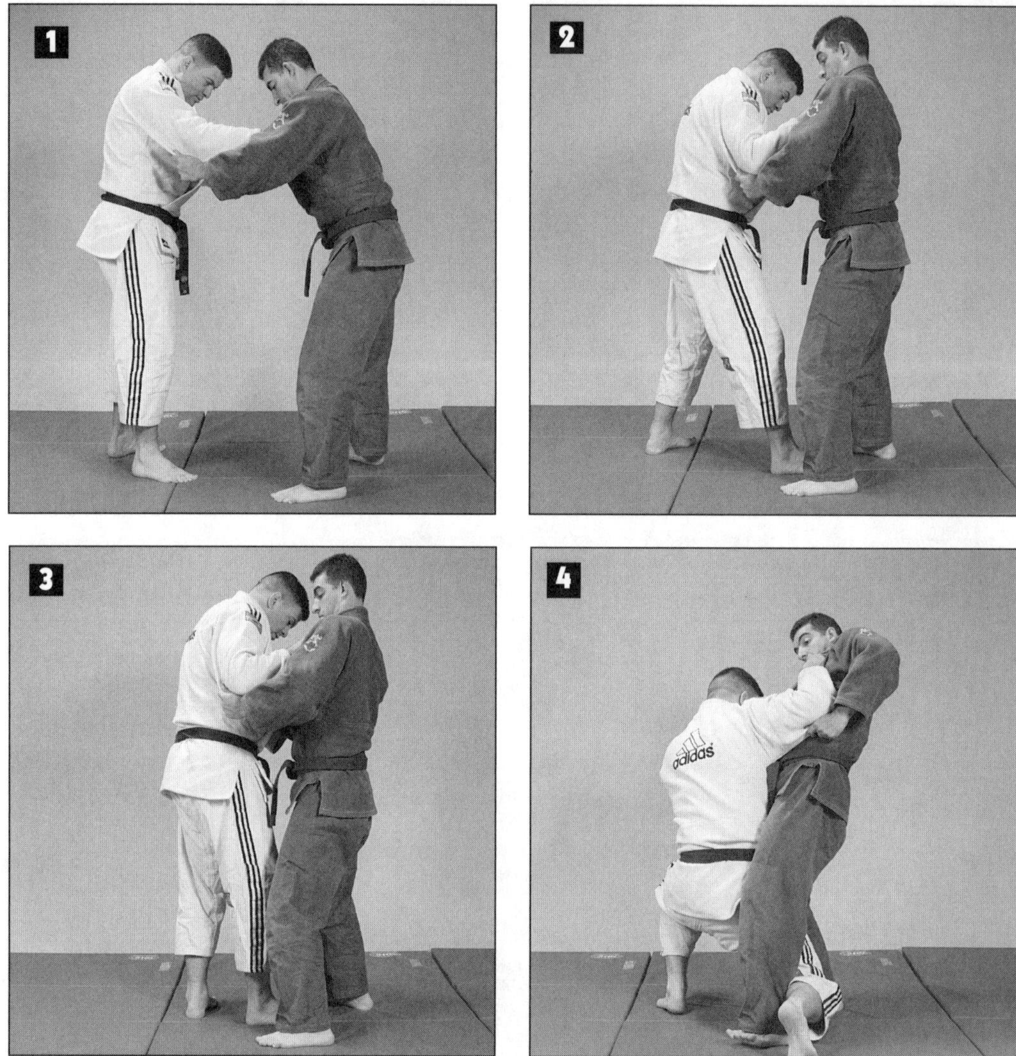

Rigan adopts the orthodox right-handed sleeve and lapel grip (1). To again create pressure and prepare for the inside sweep, Rigan moves his right foot forward (2) and then his left (3). Again, note how close he is to his opponent.

As he begins to execute the sweep (4), the opponent feels the entry action and lifts his left leg (5), escaping the sweep (6).

continued

continued from page 13

Rigan then moves his left leg to the front (7) and grabs the opponent's right leg with both arms (8). He pulls the leg up (9), unbalancing the opponent (10).

Takedowns and Throws 5

Once the opponent hits the floor, Rigan can go for a finishing technique (11).

1
2
3
4
5
6

Rigan takes a firm hold on his opponent's right sleeve and left lapel (1). While raising the right arm, Rigan moves his right arm to his adversary's right hip while simultaneously moving his right leg close to the opponent's right foot (2). He grabs the opponent's right arm, moves his left leg in front of the opponent's left leg (3) and lowers his hips (4). He then throws his opponent (5-7), who lands hard on the ground (8).

Note: Your feet should be right in front of the opponent's at the time you are ready to bring your hips down for the throw. The four feet should create a "square." This will ensure that you have the correct leverage in the technique.

Rigan latches onto the opponent's right sleeve and left side of the lapel (1). He raises his adversary's right arm, slides his right arm in front of his opponent and moves his right foot next to the opponent's right foot (2). Once he grabs the opponent's right arm, he moves his left leg in front of the opponent's left leg (3). To get more leverage for the throw, he places his knees on the ground (4) and executes the throw (5-6).

By lowering himself, he brings his opponent closer to the ground, and this facilitates the posterior throw and control (7).

1
2
3
4
5
6

Takedowns and Throws 8

7

8

9

Rigan adopts the orthodox left-handed sleeve and lapel grip (1). He forces his opponent's right arm down (2), releases the grip, swings his arm under and moves his left foot near the adversary's left foot (3). Once he has grabbed the opponent's left arm, he shifts his body and moves his right leg in front of the opponent's right foot (4). He lowers his hips (5) so he can start the throw (6) over his left shoulder (7). The opponent lands firmly on the ground (8-9).

Rigan adopts the orthodox right-handed sleeve and lapel grip (1). Then he releases his grip with his left hand and quickly grabs the opponent's right wrist (2). He forces the opponent's right arm down and away (3-4) and eventually breaks the grip.

Takedowns and Throws 9

Once the grip is broken, Rigan moves his left leg in front of the opponent's left foot (5) and simultaneously grabs the left arm while he places his right foot in front of the opponent's right foot (6).

continued

continued from page 23

He lowers his right knee to the floor (7) and then the left (8), so he can throw his opponent onto the ground (9-12).

Takedowns and Throws 9

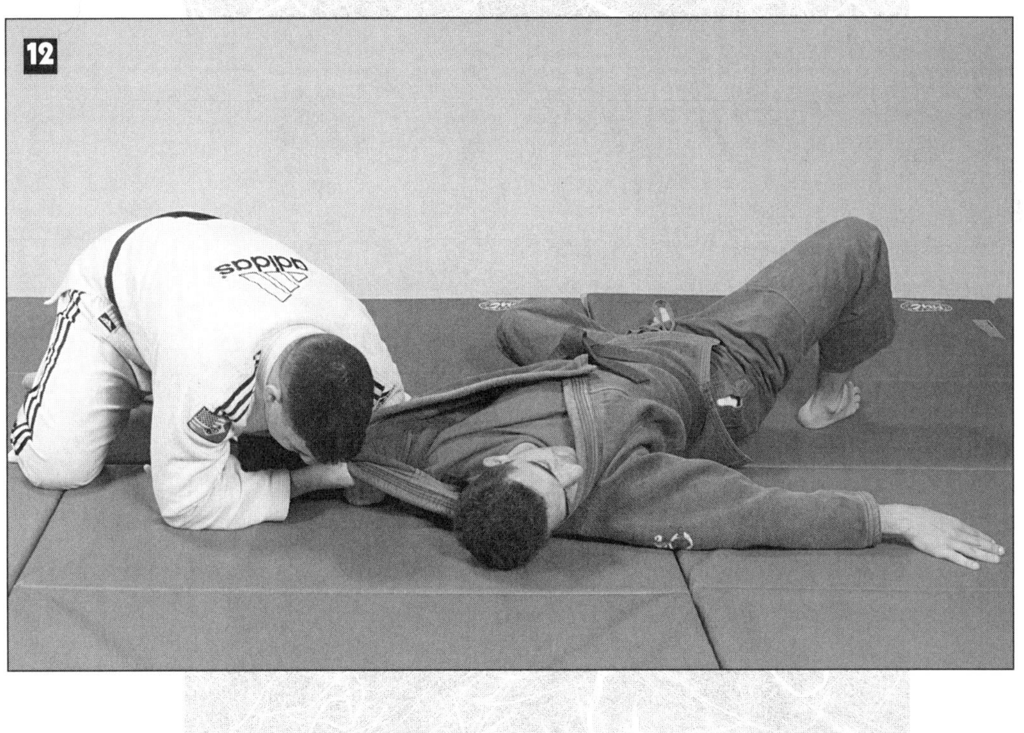

Rigan adopts the orthodox right-handed sleeve and lapel grip (1). He pulls his opponent's arms up (2) and ducks his head under the opponent's right armpit (3).

Takedowns and Throws 10

He quickly grabs both of the opponent's legs (4). Using his right shoulder to apply pressure (5),

continued

continued from page 27

Rigan pushes his opponent hard (6) and sends him sprawling through the air (7-8).

Once his opponent hits the ground (9), Rigan can start the offensive (10).

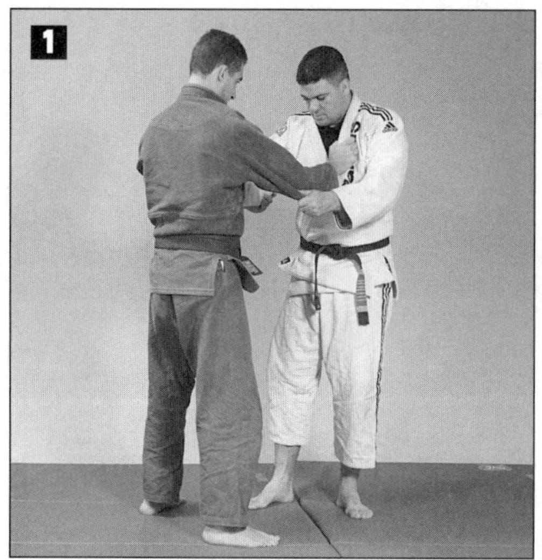

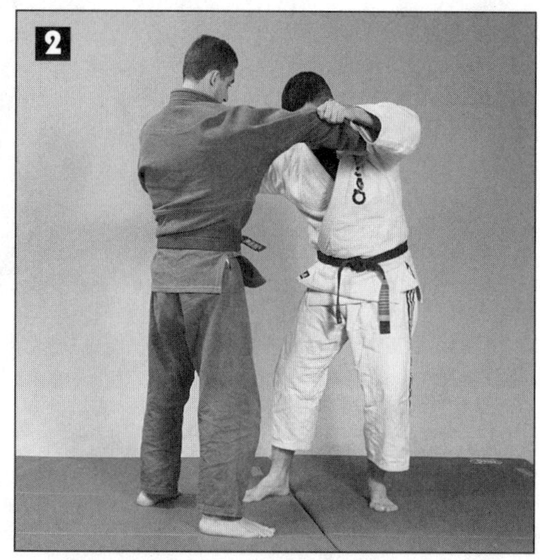

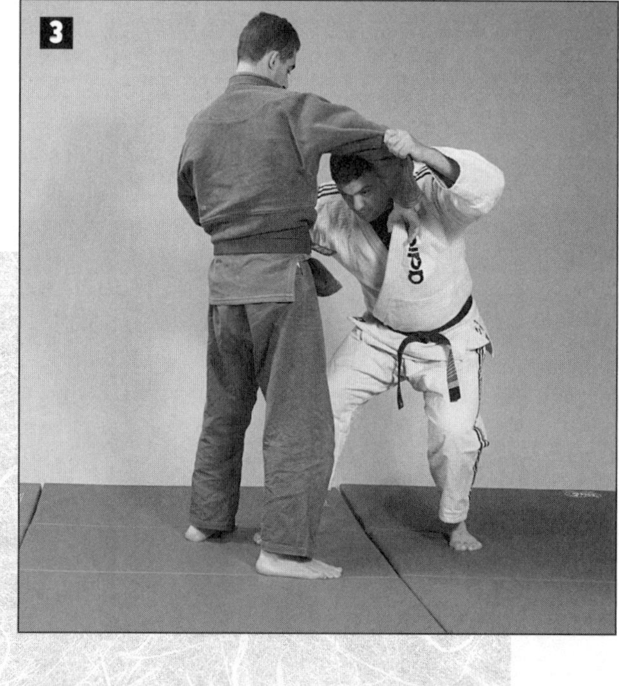

Rigan uses the orthodox right-handed sleeve and lapel grip (1). He pulls up with both hands (2) and moves his head under his opponent's right armpit (3).

Takedowns and Throws 11

Then he quickly grabs both of the opponent's legs (4). Rigan puts his right foot behind his opponent's left foot (5)

continued

continued from page 31

and pushes (6) until he can hook the right leg from behind (7). Now he can use his weight (8) to unbalance the opponent, and

Takedowns and Throws 11

take him to the ground (9). Here he can fully control him with his body and arms (10).

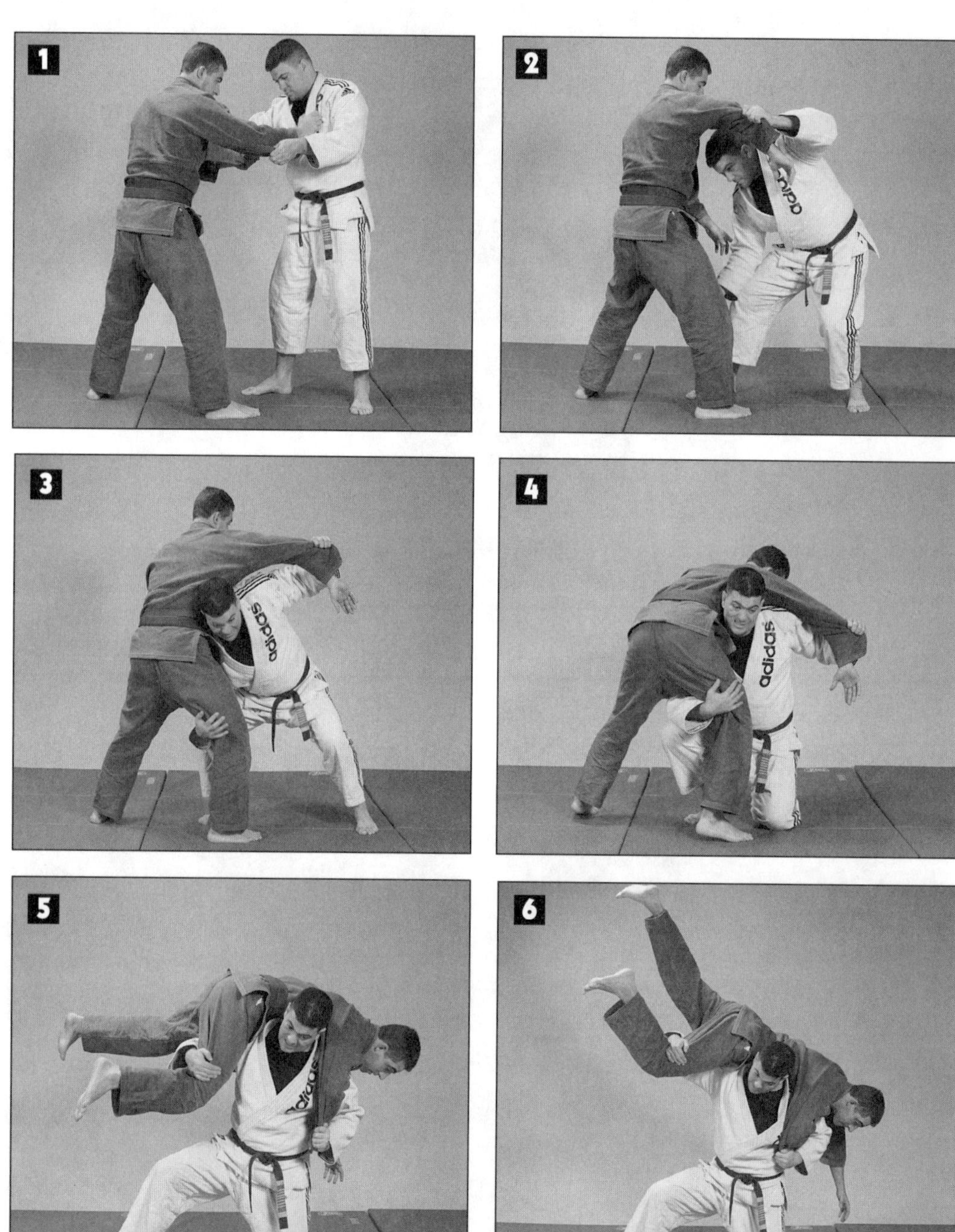
1
2
3
adidas
4
adidas
5
6

Takedowns and Throws 12

Rigan grabs his opponent's right sleeve and left side of the lapel (1). He releases the grip with his right hand (2), grabs the opponent's right leg (3) and simultaneously puts his left knee on the ground (4). He maintains control of the opponent's sleeve, so he can easily pull him over his shoulder (5),

and throw him to the other side (6-7). Then, he controls him on the ground and starts his offensive (8).

Rigan adopts the orthodox right-handed sleeve and lapel grip (1). Rigan turns his left elbow to the inside (2) and moves it under the opponent's right arm (3). This creates an opening for Rigan to pass his head under the arm (4).

Takedowns and Throws 13

Simultaneously, he drops his right knee onto the floor and shoots his right arm between the opponent's legs (5). Creating a strong base, he uses his left leg (6)

continued

continued from page 37

to lower his body (7) and unbalance the opponent, who falls forward over his right shoulder (8-9).

By turning to his left, Rigan brings the opponent onto the ground (10).

Rigan employs the orthodox right-handed sleeve and lapel grip (1). He releases the grip, grabs the opponent's right wrist and pushes it down (2). He releases his hold, lowers his left knee onto the floor and grabs the opponent's left leg with his left arm (3). By pulling with his right hand, Rigan unbalances the opponent (4), and

starts to throw him over his shoulders (5-6). When the opponent hits the ground, Rigan initiates the offensive for the submission (7).

1

2

3

4

5

6

Takedowns and Throws 15

Rigan utilizes the orthodox right-handed sleeve and lapel grip (1). He releases the grip with his right hand and extends his arm over the opponent's left shoulder (2). He moves his left foot to the side and shifts his body closer to the opponent (3). While maintaining a tight grip on the opponent's right sleeve, Rigan raises his right leg (4) to prepare the sweep (5-6).

The adversary becomes airborne (7), lands on the ground and Rigan quickly controls him (8).

Rigan adopts the orthodox right-handed sleeve and lapel grip (1). Rigan releases the collar, moves his arm over the opponent's left shoulder and grabs the gi (2). He moves his left foot to the side and brings his body close to the opponent so he can initiate a sweep with his right leg (3). The opponent blocks the attempt, so Rigan lowers his right knee to the ground (4).

While dropping down, he pulls down hard with his arms, which sends the opponent onto the floor (5-6). Rigan can now start the final offensive (7).

1
2
3
4
5
6

Takedowns and Throws 17

Rigan adopts the orthodox right-handed sleeve and lapel grip (1). Rigan pulls the sleeve with his left hand (2) and moves his right elbow under the opponent's right armpit without releasing the grip (3). He uses precise footwork to place himself in the proper position in front of the opponent (4). He lowers his body (5) and begins a throw (6) that sends the opponent flying (7).

The adversary lands on the ground (8).

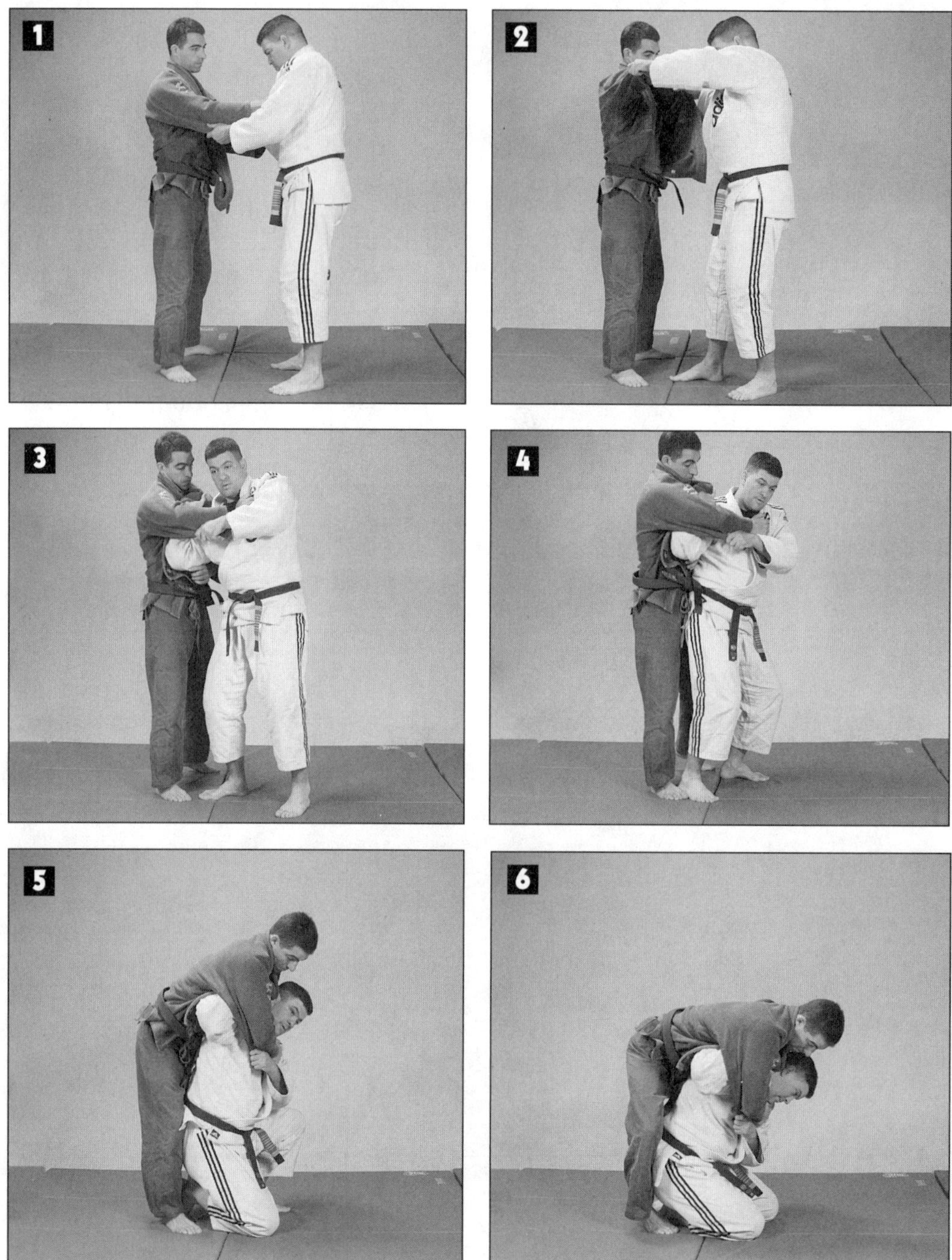
1
2
3
4
5
6

Takedowns and Throws 18

Rigan again grabs the opponent's right sleeve and left side of the lapel (1). Rigan pulls the sleeve with his left hand (2) and moves his right elbow under the opponent's right armpit without releasing the grip (3). He uses precise footwork to place his hips in the proper position in front of the opponent (4). Rigan drops his right knee to the ground (5) and then his left (6), which unbalances the opponent.

He can now throw his opponent over his right shoulder (7). Once the adversary is on the ground, Rigan goes for the final submission (8).

Rigan faces his opponent (1). He initiates the offensive by stepping forward with his right leg (2) and lowering his body (3) so he can shoot in uncontested (4).

Takedowns and Throws 19

He grabs both legs (5) and puts his right knee on the floor to establish a base (6).

continued

continued from page 51

Once the base is strong, Rigan moves his left foot to the side (7) and turns to the right (8). This unbalances the opponent (9),

Takedowns and Throws 19

sending him to the ground (10). Rigan then goes for the submission (11).

11

1
2
3
4
5
6

Takedowns and Throws 20

The opponent grabs Rigan's gi with his right hand (1). Rigan uses both hands to push the opponent's hand, which breaks the hold (2).

Rigan passes his left hand behind the opponent's back and grabs the belt, as he simultaneously pulls the sleeve with his right hand (3). He inserts his left leg between the opponent's (4) and drops to the ground to throw the aggressor off balance (5). By pulling with his left hand and using the left leg, Rigan sweeps his opponent (6), taking him to the ground (7). He can now initiate the offensive (8).

The opponent unsuccessfully attempts to grab Rigan (1). Next, Rigan takes a step forward, grabs the opponent's belt (2) and pulls back to unbalance him (3). Rigan inserts his right leg between the opponent's (4), pulls back and throws him (5).

Takedowns and Throws 21

Once his opponent hits the ground, Rigan turns, controls him (6) and takes the initiative to attack (7).

The opponent grabs Rigan's left collar (1). Rigan moves back (2) and uses both hands to break the grip (3). He turns to the right, takes a step forward with his left foot (4) and simultaneously twists the opponent's arm as he

applies pressure on the elbow (5). If he continues to crank on the armlock (6), Rigan can take his opponent down (6).

Using the orthodox right-handed sleeve and lapel grip, Rigan grabs his opponent (1). He then takes a step forward with his right foot (2) and lowers his left knee onto the ground (3). By dropping to the ground, Rigan throws the opponent's balance off (4). Rigan inserts his right leg under the opponents left leg (5)

to sweep the opponent over his body (6). By keeping his knee on the opponent's stomach, Rigan can start the offensive to gain a submission (7).

1
2
3
4
5
6

Takedowns and Throws 24

Rigan adopts the orthodox right-handed sleeve and lapel grip (1). He releases the grip with his right hand (2), reaches around the opponent's neck and grabs the opposite side of the collar (3). Using precise footwork, Rigan places his hips in front of the opponent (4), drops his weight (5) and throws the opponent over his right side (6-7).

By keeping tight control of the opponent's right hand, Rigan is ready to initiate the attack on the ground (8).

Rigan adopts the orthodox right-handed sleeve and lapel grip (1). He releases the grip with his right hand (2), reaches around the opponent's neck and grabs the opposite side of the collar. Rigan moves his right leg in front of the opponent's right side (3) and "flips" his hips to throw his adversary's balance off (4). By dropping his right knee (5),

Takedowns and Throws 25

Rigan throws his opponent onto the ground (6), where he follows up with a side control (7).

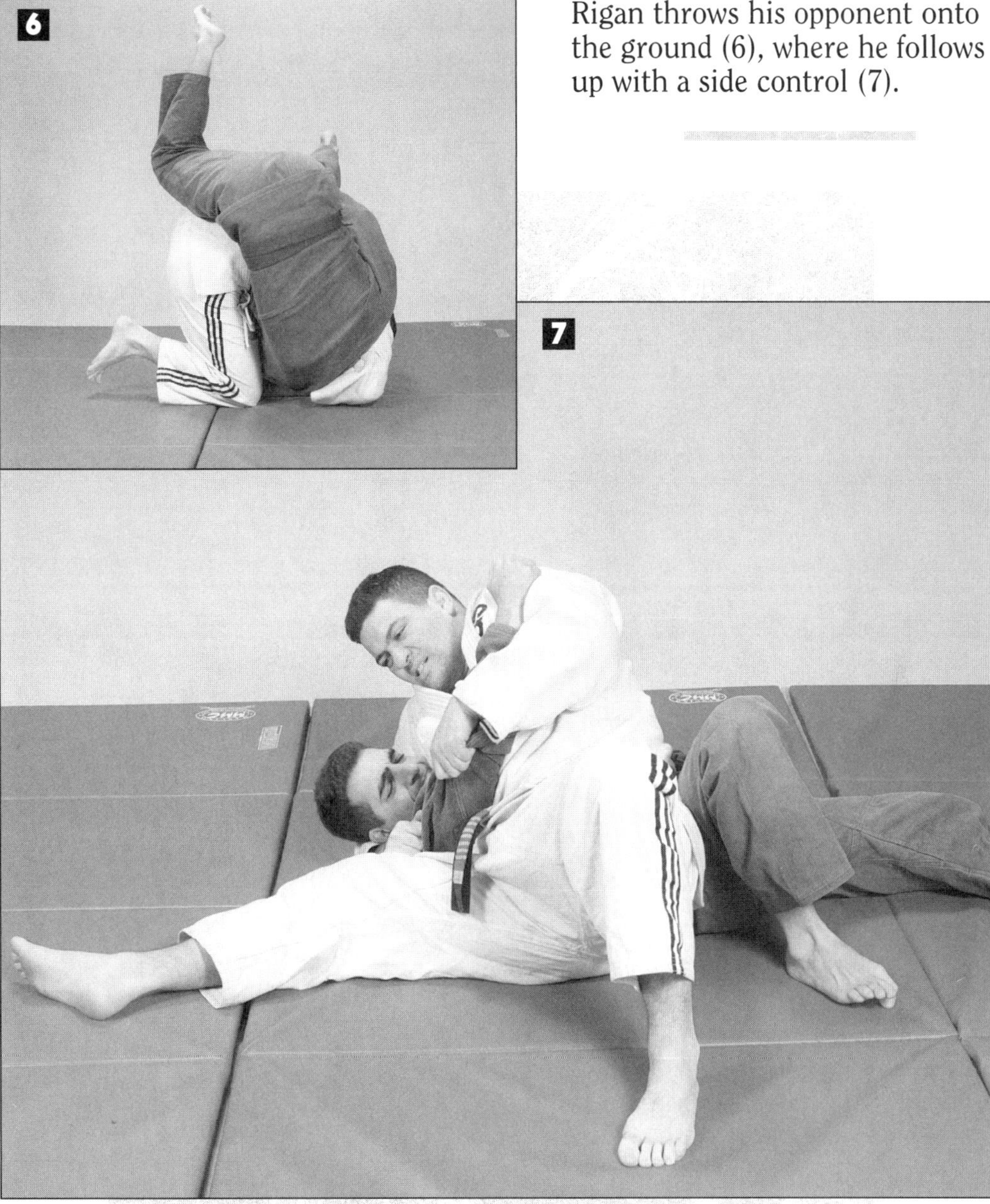

Rigan faces his opponent (1). As soon as the opponent tries to close the distance, Rigan grabs the aggressor's right wrist with his left hand (2). Next, he grabs the opponent's right elbow with his right hand (3). With full control of the opponent's right arm, Rigan side steps to the left as he releases the grip with his left hand (4) so he can grab the opponent's waist (5),

and take him to the ground (6).

Using his right hand, the opponent grabs Rigan (1). In response, Rigan reaches over the opponent's right arm, grabs the collar (2) and shifts his feet so he is closer (3). Rigan raises his left leg (4) and throws his body into the air, as he simultaneously puts his right leg behind the opponent's legs (5).

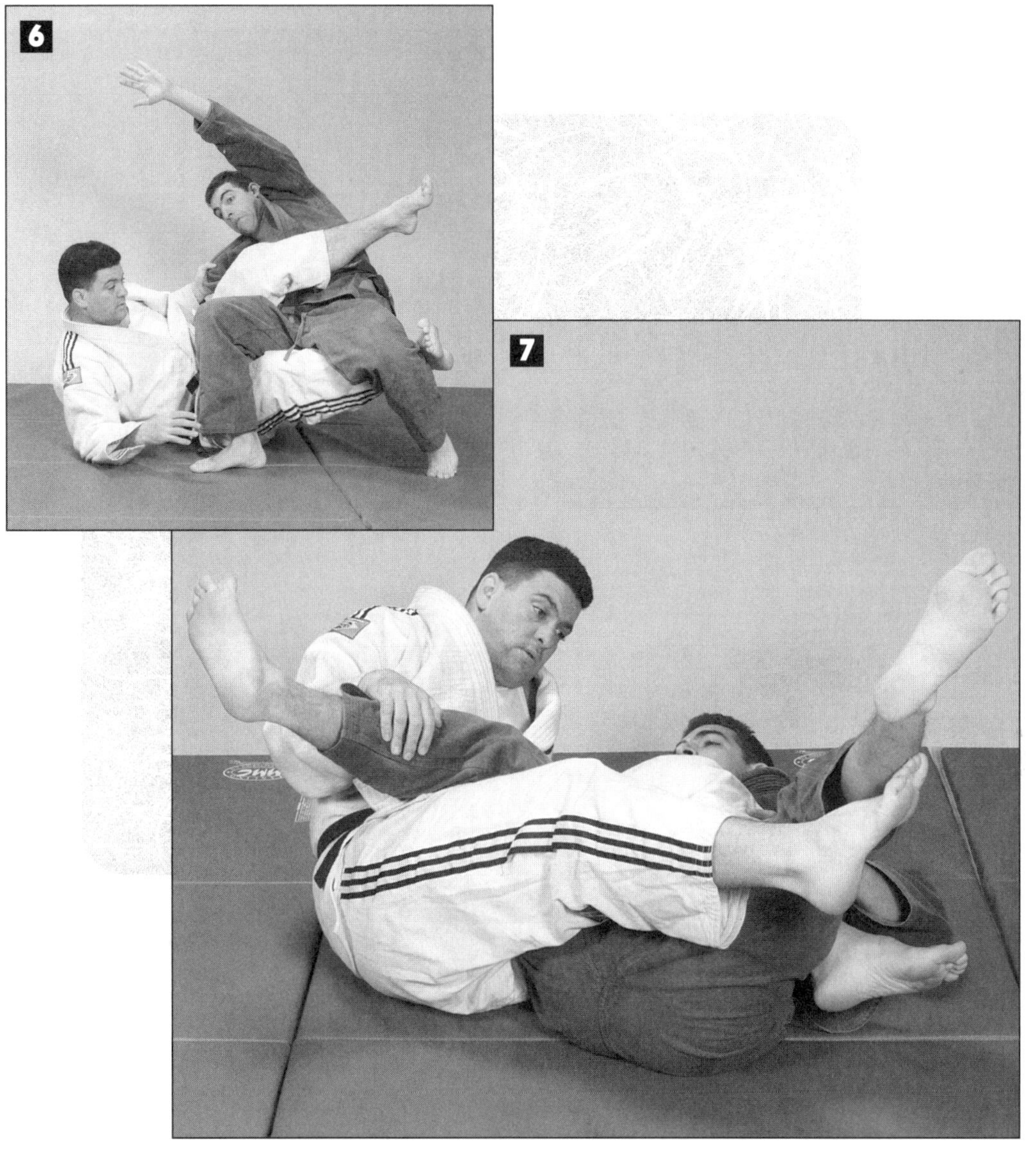

This unbalances the aggressor (6) and sends him to the ground. Rigan can now initiate the offensive (7).

Rigan and his opponent assume the orthodox right-handed sleeve and lapel grip (1). Rigan brings his hips forward (2) and drops onto the ground without releasing his grip (3).

This allows him to control the opponent from the bottom position (4) and apply an armlock (5).

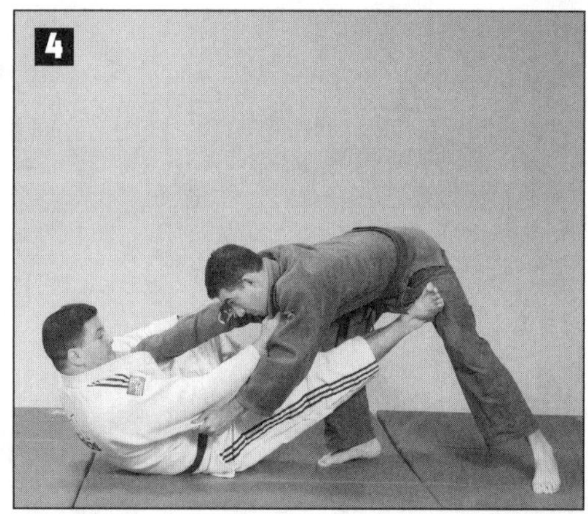

Both fighters adopt the orthodox right-handed sleeve and lapel grip (1). Rigan moves forward, and using his right leg (2), pushes the opponent's left leg (3). This unbalances the opponent. Rigan drops to the ground (4),

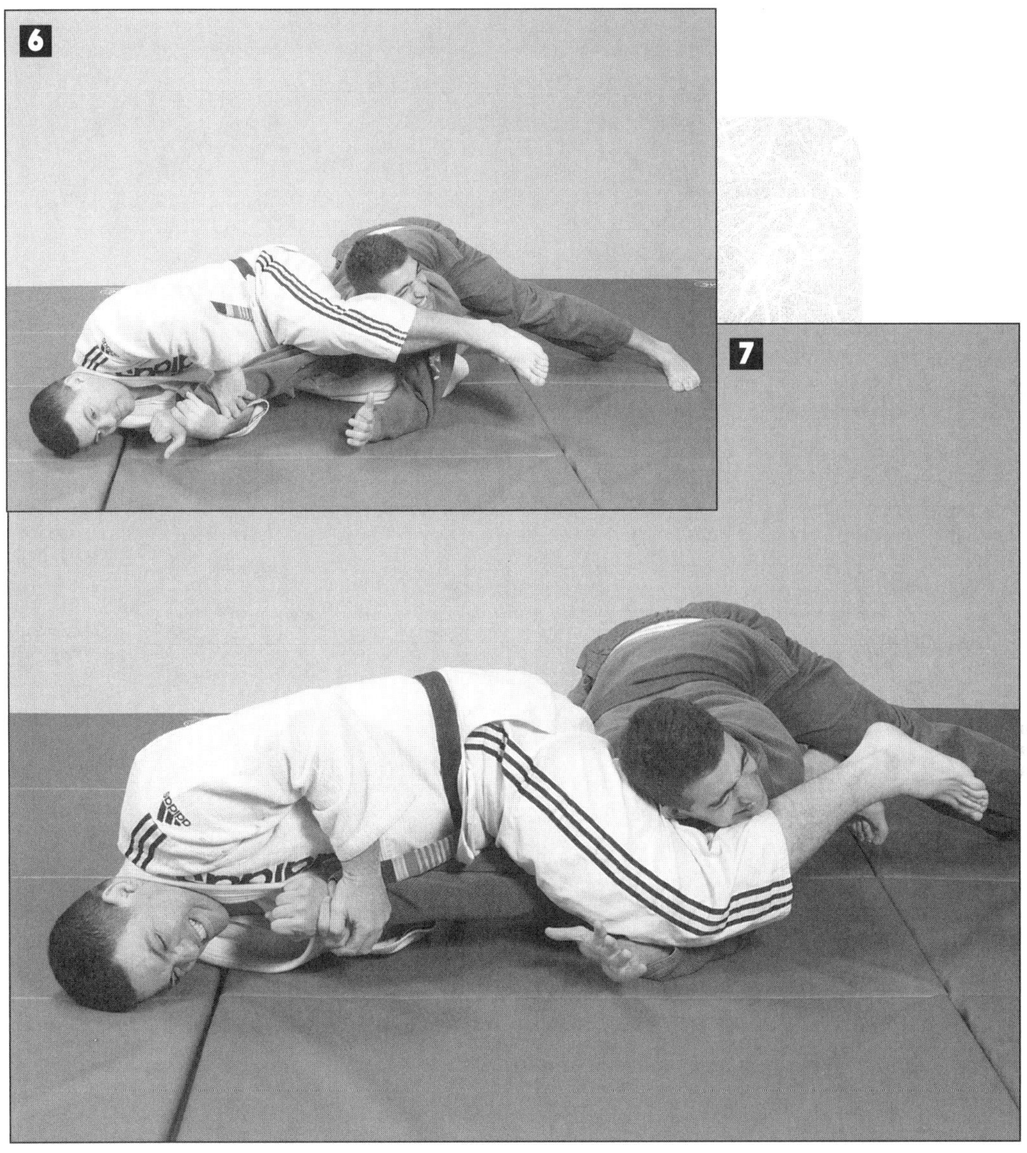

passes his left leg over the opponent's head (5-6) and applies a straight armlock (7).

1
2
3
4
5
6

Takedowns and Throws 30

The opponent grabs Rigan with his right arm (1). Rigan moves his left foot forward and grabs the left side of the opponent's collar with his right hand (2). When the opponent tries to move away (3), Rigan pulls him back (4). Using his right leg, Rigan hits the opponent's shin (5), sweeps him (6),

and throws him to the right (7). Once his adversary is down, Rigan controls him and initiates the offensive for the submission (8).

Rigan and his opponent adopt the orthodox right-handed sleeve and lapel grip (1). Rigan moves his right foot forward and circles with his left. This throws the opponent off balance (2). He moves his right leg between the opponent's (3), leans to roll forward (4), grabs the opponent's left ankle and tumbles (5).

Takedowns and Throws 31

Without releasing the grip, Rigan rolls all the way over (6) and finishes with a straight kneebar (7).

Both fighters adopt the orthodox right-handed sleeve and lapel grip (1). Rigan releases the grip from the lapel, grabs the opponent's back (2) and closes the distance with his right foot (3). He aligns the hips (4) and throws his opponent over his right side (5-6).

Once the adversary is on the ground, Rigan begins the offensive with a knee-on-the-stomach side control (7).

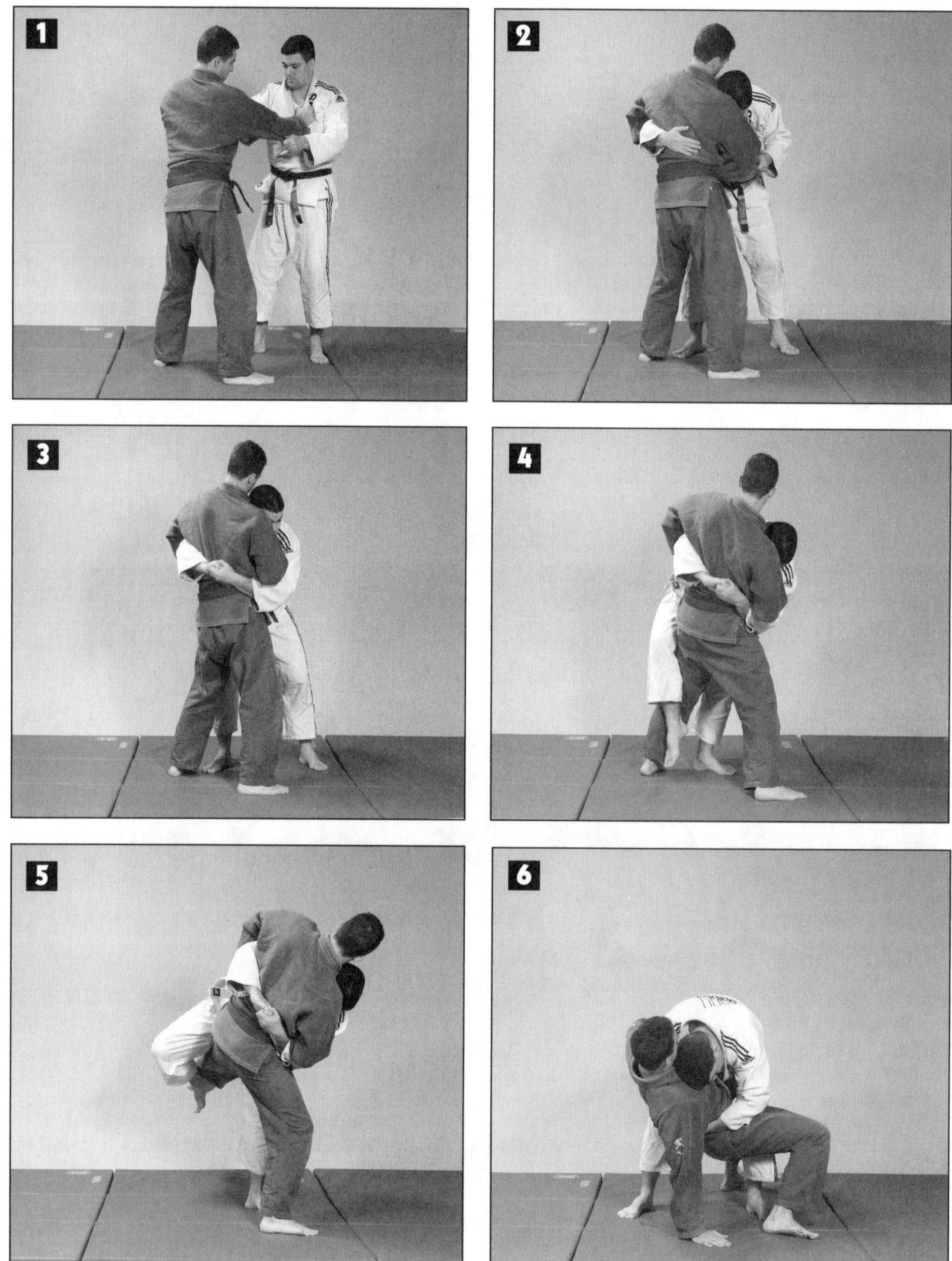
1
2
3
4
5
6

Takedowns and Throws 33

Both fighters adopt the orthodox right-handed sleeve and lapel grip (1). Rigan releases the lapel, grabs the opponent's back (2) and latches his hands together (3). Immediately, he hooks the opponent's left leg with his right leg (4) and pulls hard as he simultaneously pushes forward with his body (5). This knocks the opponent off balance (6),

and sends him to the floor (7). Rigan mounts him for a final control (8).

Rigan and his opponent assume the orthodox right-handed sleeve and lapel grip (1). Rigan moves backwards to create space (2) and prepares to drop to the floor (3). Once he's down, he places his right foot on the opponent's stomach (4). Rigan leans back, pulls with both hands, keeps a tight grip and sends his opponent into the air (5-6).

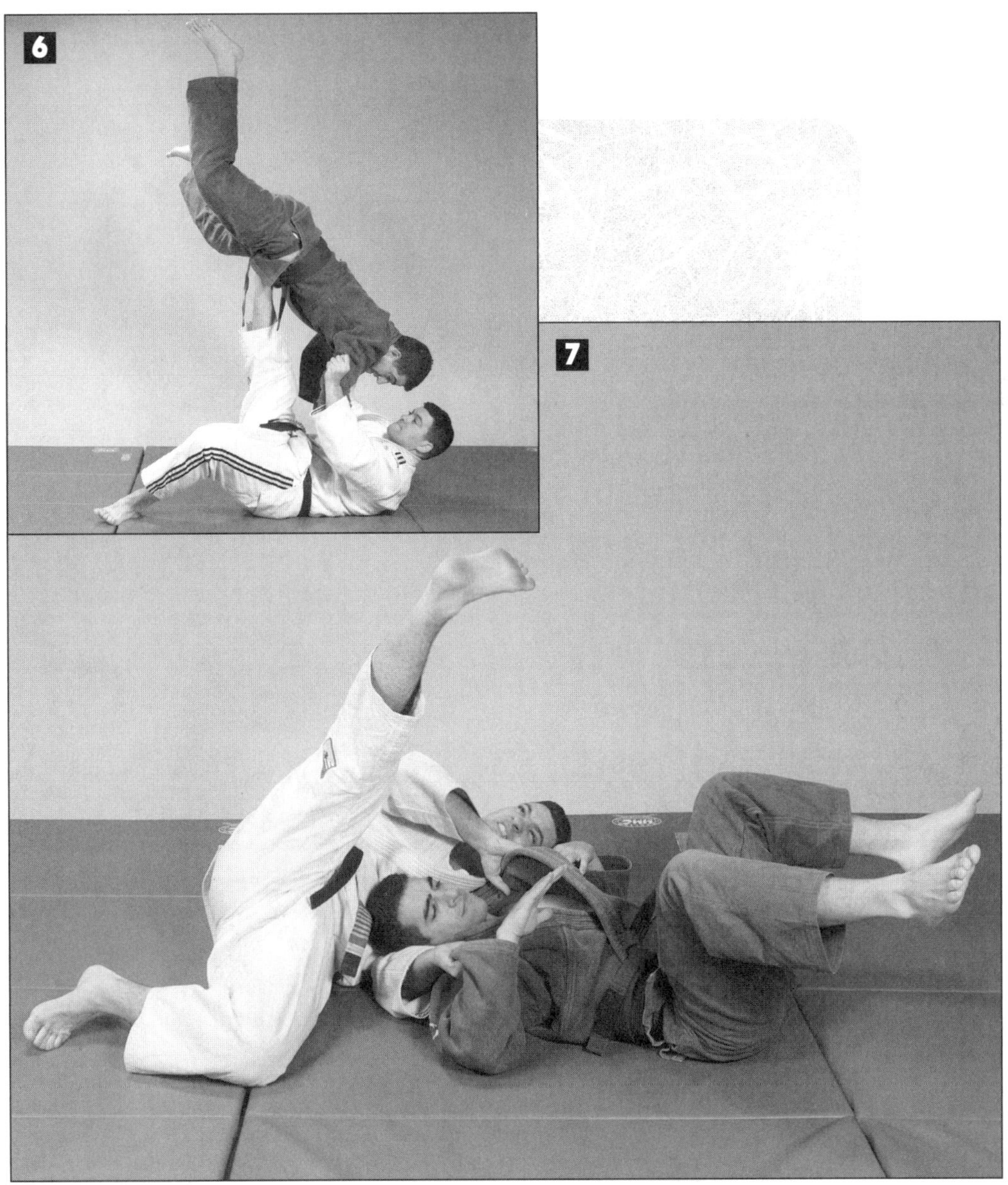

When his opponent hits the ground, Rigan can take the offensive (7).

1

2

3

4

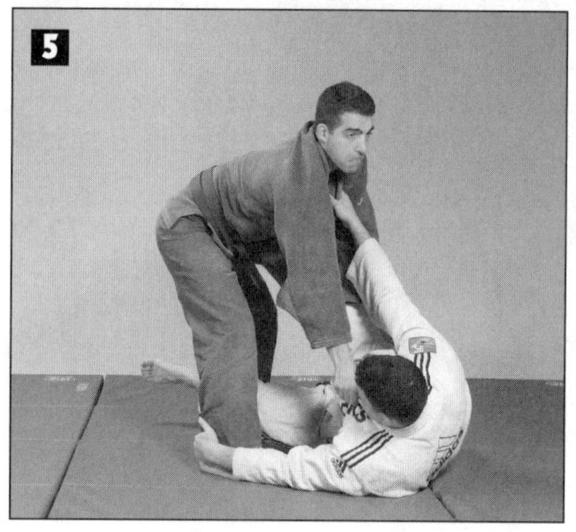
5

6

Takedowns and Throws 35

Rigan and his opponent adopt the orthodox right-handed sleeve and lapel grip (1). Rigan moves backwards to create space and build momentum (2). He drops to the floor and places his right foot on the opponent's stomach (3).

The opponent realizes what Rigan is trying to do, so he lowers his hips to prevent the maneuver (4). Rigan reacts by sliding his hips forward, grabbing the opponent's right ankle, (5) pulling hard with his left hand and simultaneously pushing the opponent's right hip (6). This brings the opponent onto the ground (7), where Rigan initiates the offensive (8).

Rigan and his opponent adopt the orthodox right-handed sleeve and lapel grip (1). Next, Rigan swings his leg to create momentum (2). He drops down and puts his left foot on the opponent's right hip (3). Taking advantage of the momentum, he pushes the opponent into the air (4-5),

and throws him to the left (6). Rigan can now start the offensive toward the submission (7).

Rigan faces his opponent (1). Suddenly, he drops (2) and initiates the offensive by grabbing the opponent's left ankle with his right hand (3) and then his left (4). Using both hands enables him to maintain tighter control.

Takedowns and Throws 37

This allows him to create a base to push with his right shoulder (5), knocking the opponent down while maintaining control of his left leg (6).

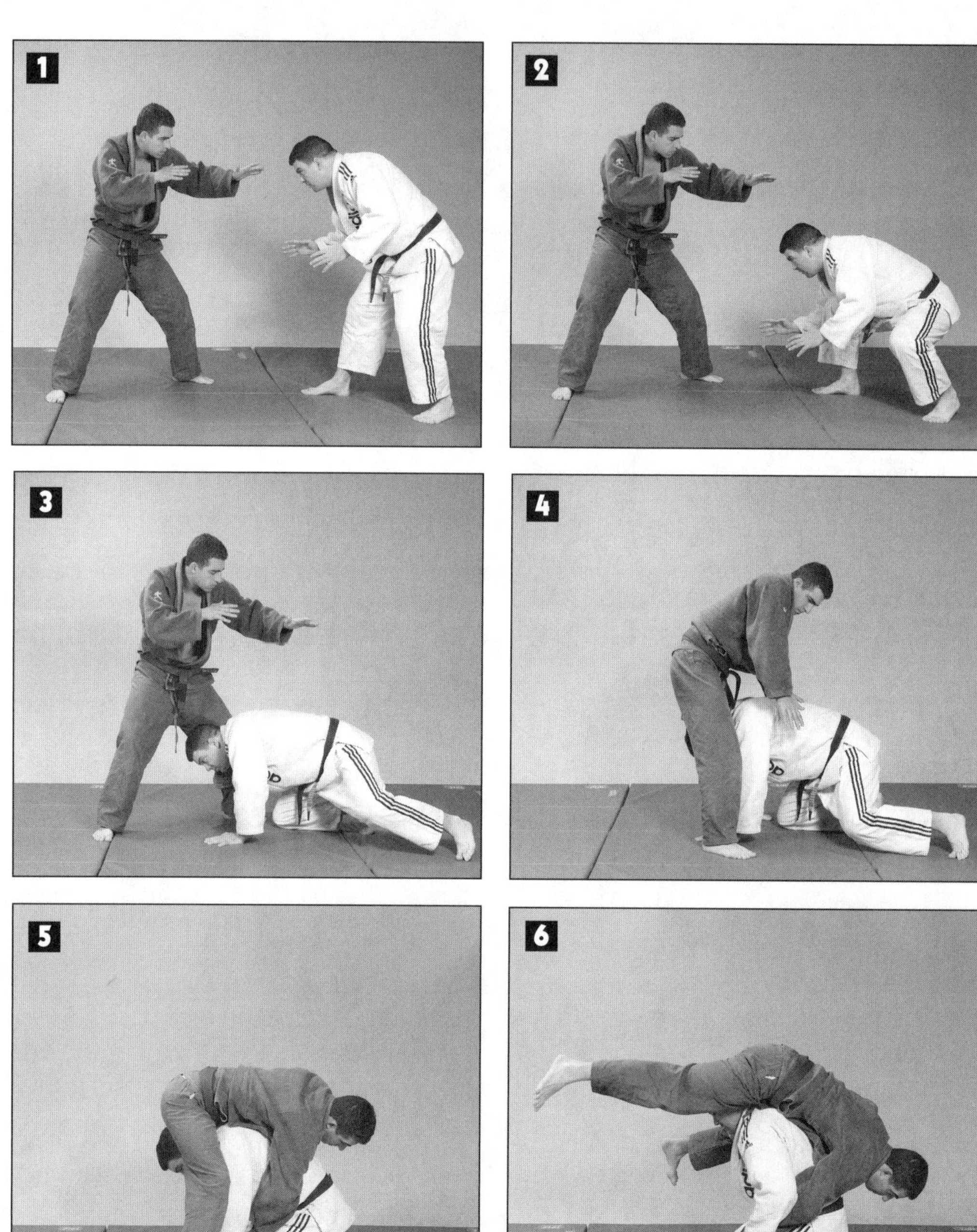
1
2
3
4
5
6

Takedowns and Throws 38

Rigan faces his opponent (1). He suddenly drops his body (2) and initiates the offensive by grabbing the opponent's left ankle (3). The opponent steps forward with his right leg (4) and tries to grab and control Rigan from the top (5). Rigan begins to sit up and this throws the opponent's balance off (6). This maneuver allows him to grab the opponent's left leg (7). Rigan twists to the left (8) and smashes his opponent against the ground (9). Note: Always maintain control of the opponent's leg for a faster counterattack and to initiate the offense on the ground.

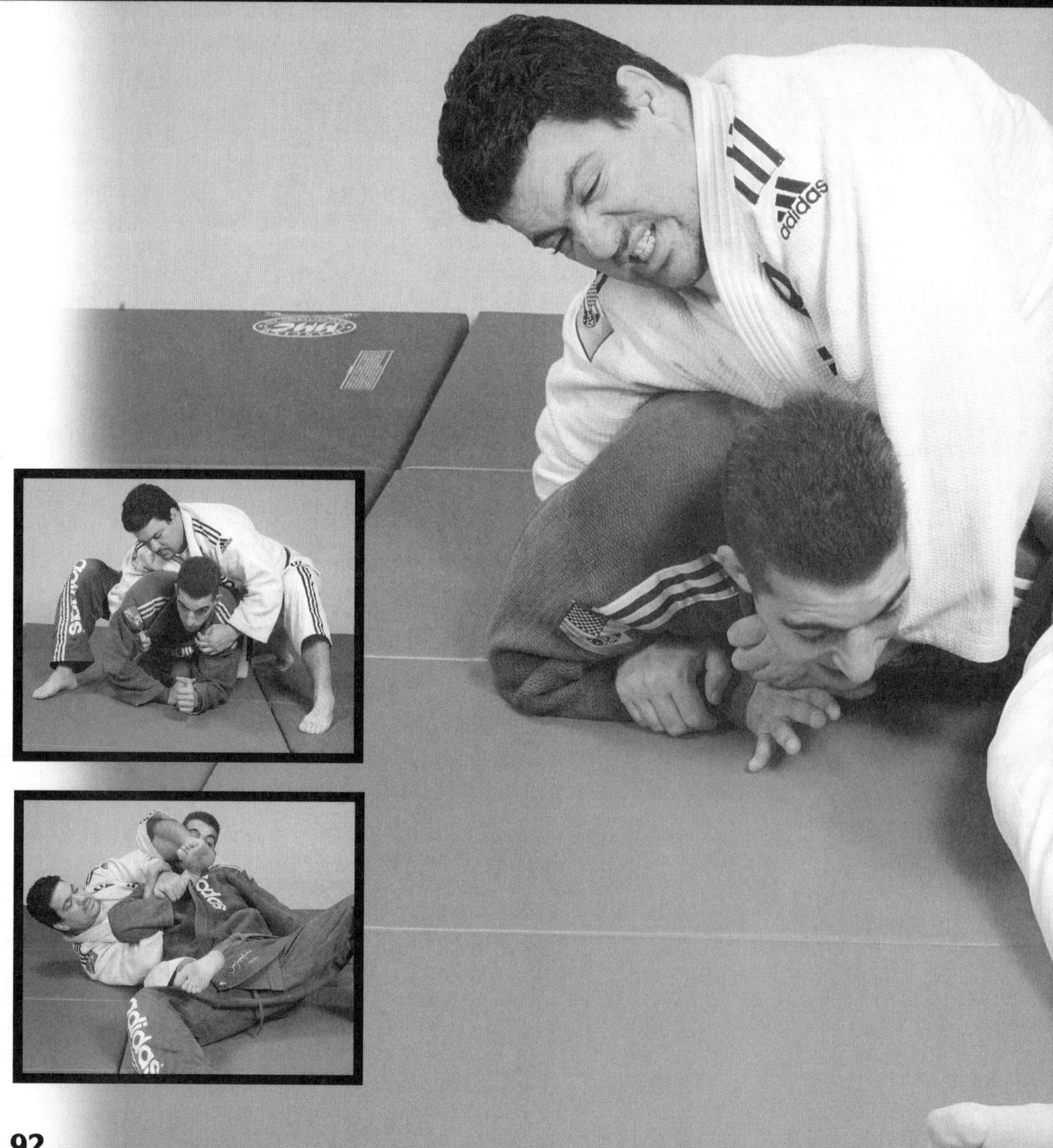

ATTACKS FROM THE BACK

VOL. 3

By holding the lapel, Rigan controls his opponent from behind (1). He releases the left-handed grip and slides his hand to the right side of the collar (2).

Attacks From The Back 1

Then he releases the opponent's lapel with his right hand and grabs the left side of the collar (3). Finally, he leans forward and applies pressure with his body to choke his opponent out (4).

Rigan controls the confrontation by holding his opponent's lapel (1). He releases the grip on the left side and slides his hand to the collar (2). This time he uses his right hand — not to grab the opposite side of the collar — but to control the opponent's right hand (3).

Attacks From The Back 2

Rigan leans forward and starts putting pressure on his opponent (4). To create leverage and increase the pressure, Rigan moves his right leg forward. Now he can apply a choke (5).

Rigan controls his opponent from behind by holding the lapel (1). Once again, he releases the grip on the left side and latches onto the collar (2). He hooks his right arm under the opponent's right leg and exerts pressure on him by leaning forward (3).

Attacks From The Back 3

Rigan moves his right leg forward (4) and applies additional pressure for the choke (5).

Rigan initiates the attack from behind (1). He grabs the opponent's left arm (2) and shoves it between his legs (3). By leaning forward, he puts pressure on the opponent's chest (4). Note how he simultaneously hooks the right arm. Rigan rolls forward over his right shoulder (5),

falls on the other side of his opponent (6) and applies a choke (7). To execute the choke, he grabs the opponent's lapel with his left hand and creates leverage with his legs and right arm.

1
2
3
4
5
6

Attacks From The Back 5

Rigan initiates the attack from the back (1). He grabs the opponent's left arm (2) and forces it between his legs (3). As he hooks the right arm, Rigan leans forward and puts pressure on the adversary's chest (4).

Rigan rolls over his right shoulder (5), falls on the other side (6) and reaches for the opponent's collar with his left hand (7). Note that he reaches in front — not from behind — as he did in the previous technique. He executes the choke and prevents the opponent from escaping by controlling both arms (8).

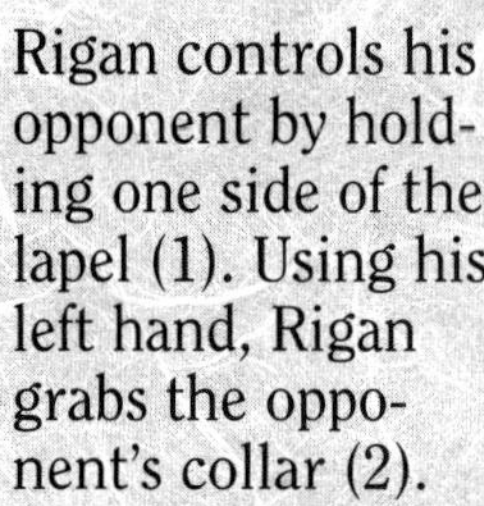

Rigan controls his opponent by holding one side of the lapel (1). Using his left hand, Rigan grabs the opponent's collar (2).

Attacks From The Back 6

Next, he lifts his left leg over the opponent's head (3). To execute the choke (4), Rigan wraps his leg around the back of the opponent's head and pulls with his left hand and pushes with his left leg.

To control the confrontation, Rigan latches onto the back of the adversary's collar and right arm (1). Rigan moves his left hand around the opponent's neck without releasing the grip on the collar (2). This makes the gi choke the opponent, especially when Rigan leans forward and applies more pressure to the back (3).

Attacks From The Back 7

Next, Rigan twists his body so he can slide his head under the right arm and then he grabs the opponent's left arm and cranks on it (4). Rigan keeps turning until he's flat on his back, and this enables him to choke his opponent out (5).

Rigan controls the opponent from behind. Again he has both hands on the lapel (1). Rigan releases the lapel with his right hand and grabs the upper portion of the collar (2).

Attacks From The Back 8

Rigan chokes the opponent (3).

Rigan controls the opponent from behind with both hands on the lapel (1). Rigan again releases the grip with his right hand and grabs the upper left portion of the collar (2).

Attacks From The Back 

He releases the lapel with his left hand (3), slides his left arm along the side of the opponent's neck and chokes him (4).

While sitting, Rigan controls the opponent from behind. He starts passing his right arm across the neck until the tip of his elbow is in the front of the opponent's chin (1). To add pressure, he closes the angle between his forearm and biceps (2). Rigan raises his left arm over the opponent's shoulder (3). To submit his opponent, Rigan tucks his arm behind the adversary's head, places his right hand on his biceps and squeezes (4).

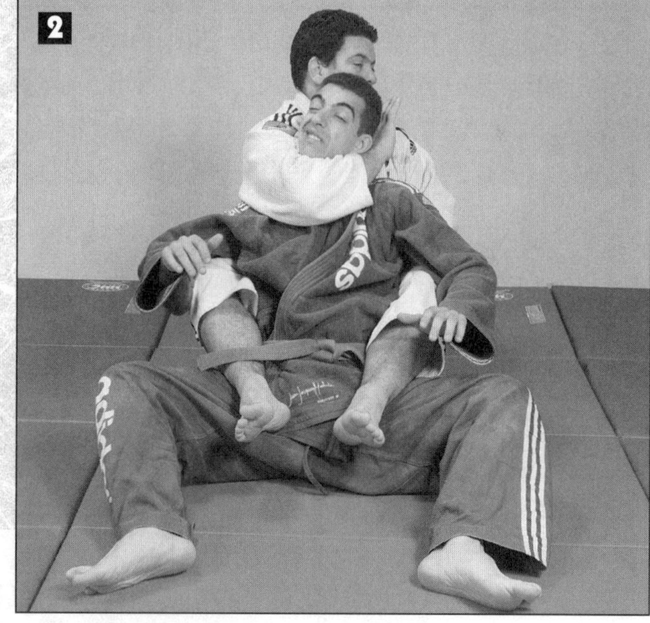

Attacks From The Back 10

Note: The initial movement (across the neck) of the right arm should apply enough pressure to make the opponent feel uncomfortable. The left hand secures and finalizes the technique. Bring your chest up to create leverage from behind. This technique doesn't need a lot of strength if properly applied. Leverage and proper angle are the key factors.

Rigan's left hand controls the lapel and his right hand the opponent's right arm (1). Rigan releases the grip with his right hand and grabs the upper portion of the collar (2).

Attacks From The Back 11

He leans backwards and grabs the opponent's left leg as he applies a submission choke (3). Note: It's vital to keep a tight grip with your right hand during the entire movement.

Rigan's left hand is on the collar, and his right hand is firmly on the adversary's right arm (1). The opponent's right arm prevents Rigan from directly applying a choke. Rigan releases the collar and grabs the opponent's right wrist. To create leverage as he falls backwards, Rigan grabs his own wrist (2).

Attacks From The Back 12

Once on the ground, Rigan lifts his left leg over the opponent's head (3), breaks the grip, places his left leg across the adversary's neck and applies a straight armlock (4). Note: To get the armlock, maintain constant pressure with both legs when breaking the grip and when pulling the opponent's arm.

With both hands on the opponent's lapel, Rigan controls the confrontation (1). To create space, Rigan moves his feet to the opponent's hips and slightly pushes forward (2).

Attacks From The Back 13

He passes his right leg over the opponent's body (3), shifts to the right (4) and applies a *triangle* from the back (5).

Rigan controls the opponent from behind. Both hands are again on the lapel (1). He releases the grip with his left hand, lifts his hand over the opponent's left shoulder and grabs the opposite side of the collar (2). To create space to raise his left leg over the opponent's shoulder, Rigan leans to his right (3).

Attacks From The Back 14

3

As he does this, he controls the adversary's right arm. Without releasing the opponent's right arm, Rigan pulls hard with his left hand, pushes with his left leg and applies a finishing choke (4).

4

While seated, Rigan controls the opponent. Both hands are on the lapel (1). He releases his left hand, pulls his arm out, slides his arm over the opponent's left shoulder and grabs the opposite side of the adversary's collar (2). As he controls the opponent's right arm, Rigan slides to his right (3).

Attacks From The Back 15

He continues to move sideways as he lifts his left shin next to the opponent's neck (4). This adds pressure and increases the leverage. Rigan pulls hard and applies the choke (5).

With his right hand on the opponent's lapel, Rigan controls the confrontation from behind (1). He releases the grip with his left hand, moves his hand over the opponent's left shoulder, grabs the opposite side of the collar and leans to his right (2).

Attacks From The Back 16

Rigan raises his left leg over the opponent's head, grabs his left foot with his right hand and applies the choke (3). The choke works because the leg works in conjunction with the established grip of the left hand.

Rigan controls the opponent, but his left leg is trapped inside the opponent's arms (1). Rigan slides to the right and uses his leg to break the grip (2). He leans more to create momentum and leverage so he can straighten the opponent's left arm (3).

Attacks From The Back 17

Rigan hooks the arm between his legs (4), turns over and pushes with his pelvis to apply a straight armlock (5).

Rigan controls the situation, but his left leg is again trapped inside the opponent's arms (1). Rigan slides his body to the side and uses his leg to break the grip (2). He leans to the side to create momentum and leverage so he can straighten the opponent's arm (3). Because the opponent is grabbing his left leg, Rigan uses his right foot to trap the arm and break the grip (4). While using his right arm for control, Rigan moves toward the adversary's head (5).

Attacks From The Back 18

Rigan rolls forward over his right shoulder (6) until he comes up on top (7). He can now apply a finishing armlock (8). Note: Grab the opponent's left leg to prevent him from rolling and escaping from the submission.

While the opponent crouches on the floor (1), Rigan stands and grabs the belt with both hands (2). Rigan lifts his opponent's hips into the air (3). While the opponent is up, Rigan inserts the "hooks" for better control (4). He immediately pushes forward with his hips and uses his left hand to prevent the opponent from stopping the action (5).

Attacks From The Back 19

Once the opponent is crushed (6), Rigan removes his left hand (7) and applies a choke from behind (8).

Rigan controls the opponent from the back. Notice that he has the "hooks" in and his right hand is on the opponent's right lapel (1). Rigan releases the grip and starts passing his left leg over the opponent's head (2-3). Once he has a secure position (4),

Attacks From The Back 20

Rigan pushes the opponent's head with the back of his leg (5). This forces the opponent onto his back. Rigan can now apply a final armlock (6).

While standing, Rigan tries to control the opponent (1). He inserts his right foot to get one "hook" in (2). The opponent prevents the second hook from going in so Rigan circles to the right and adopts a reverse position (3).

Attacks From The Back 21

Here he has easy access to the opponent's right foot (4). He grabs the opponent's foot, creates leverage with his right leg and applies a leglock (5).

ESCAPES FROM THE BACK

VOL. 3

Rigan's opponent tries to initiate the attack (1). Rigan moves his left leg to the outside as he grabs the opponent's left wrist (2). Rigan rolls over his right shoulder (3),

Escapes From The Back 1

spins to the side, switches grips (4) and brings the opponent inside his closed guard (5).

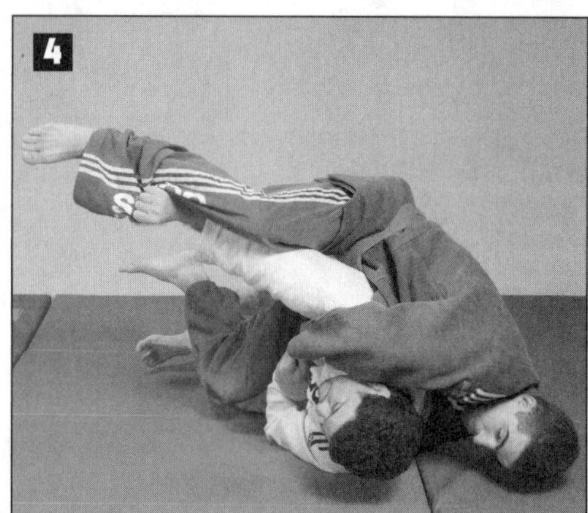

Rigan's opponent again tries to initiate the attack (1). Rigan moves his left leg to the outside as he grabs the opponent's right wrist (2). Using his right hand, Rigan grabs the opponent's right leg (3). Creating momentum with his body and controlling the opponent's right leg and left arm, Rigan sweeps him to the side (4-5),

Escapes From The Back 2

and controls him by leaning backwards (6) and by grabbing his right leg (7).

Rigan gives his back to the opponent (1). With his right hand, Rigan pushes the opponent's right hand, breaking the grip and creating space (2).

Escapes From The Back 3

This enables him to bring his left leg forward (3). By turning to the right, Rigan puts his opponent inside the closed guard (4).

Rigan is on his hands and feet as the opponent hooks his right leg (1). Rigan slides to the right and allows his right shoulder to roll, as he grabs the opponent's left leg with both hands (2).

By turning to the left, Rigan sweeps the opponent. While executing this move, he maintains control of the leg (3), so he can apply a straight leglock (4).

Rigan's opponent initiates the attack (1). Keeping his hands and feet on the ground, Rigan pushes himself up (2), rolls forward (3-5),

6

7

and escapes (6). Now he can confront his opponent from a more advantageous position (7).

The opponent controls Rigan from the back (1). Rigan uses his left hand to grab the opponent's right wrist (2). He breaks the grip and grabs his own wrist with his right hand (3).

This creates leverage when he turns to the right. He unbalances the opponent (4) and applies a bent armlock (5).

The opponent initiates the attack from the back (1). Rigan grabs the opponent's right wrist (2). This brings the opponent closer and secures the hold. Rigan uses his left hand to grab the opponent's left leg (3). Creating momentum with his body while controlling the opponent's left leg and right arm, Rigan sweeps him to the side (4-5).

Escapes From The Back 7

Here, Rigan controls the adversary by leaning backwards (6) and by grabbing his right leg (7). Now he can initiate the counterattack.

The opponent controls Rigan and tries to apply a choke from behind (1). In the process, the opponent makes the mistake of crossing both feet in front of Rigan (2). Rigan places his right foot over the opponent's feet (3). Then he puts his right foot under the back of his left knee (4), and leans backwards,

Escapes From The Back 8

creating pressure (5). By leaning to the right and stretching his body, Rigan applies a painful anklelock to his opponent (6).

The opponent tries to choke Rigan from behind (1). Rigan protects his collar with the right hand and uses his left hand to grab the opponent's right wrist (2).

Escapes From The Back 9

Rigan releases the collar, grabs his left wrist (3) and applies a straight armlock (4).

Note: When he releases his collar, Rigan slides the arm under the opponent's right arm.

Escapes From The Back 10

The opponent tries to choke Rigan from behind (1). Rigan protects his collar with his left hand, and he uses his right hand to grab the opponent's right foot (2). He moves the foot to the side (3), leans to the right (4) and throws off the opponent's balance (5). He finalizes the escape by moving his right leg outside the opponent's right leg (6). By sliding his hips (7), Rigan can begin to turn to the other side (8). This enables him to control the opponent and initiate the counterattack (9).

1

2

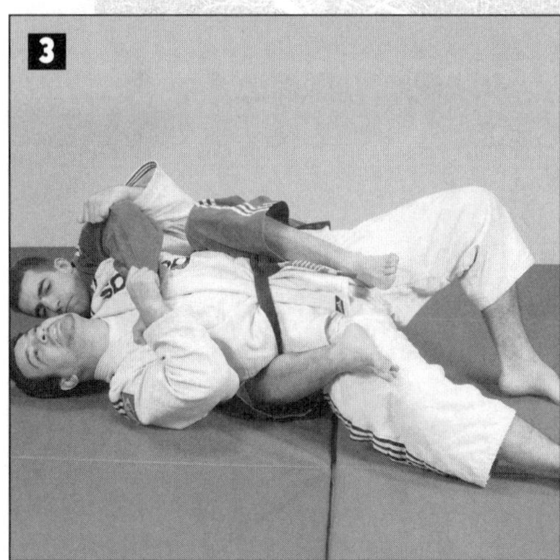
3

4

The opponent controls Rigan from the back (1). Rigan grabs the opponent's left arm and leans sideways to unbalance him (2). He arches his back and stretches his body to create leverage (3). This enables him to move his hips to the side so he can escape from the hooks (4).

Escapes From The Back 11

By grabbing the left leg, Rigan controls his opponent's position (5). Then Rigan turns sideways and brings his opponent into the open guard (6).

The opponent attacks from the back (1), but Rigan uses both hands to break the grip (2). Rigan forces the opponent's arm onto his left shoulder (3) and immediately leans back to unbalance him (4). Rigan grabs the opponent's right foot and pulls it out as he pushes upward with his hips (5).

Escapes From The Back 12

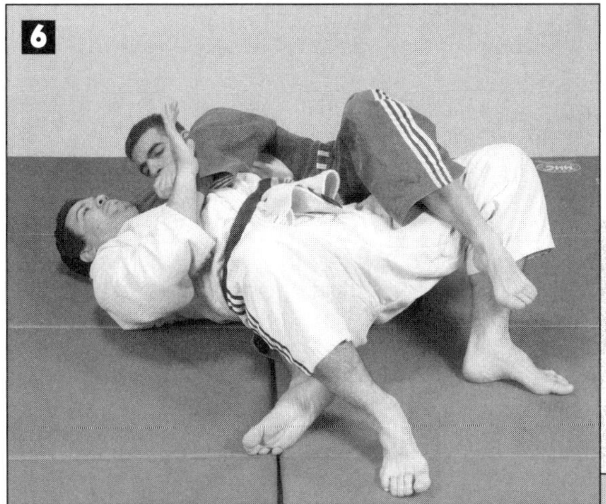

Now that he has broken the "hooks," Rigan begins to slide to the side (6) so he can initiate a counterattack (7).

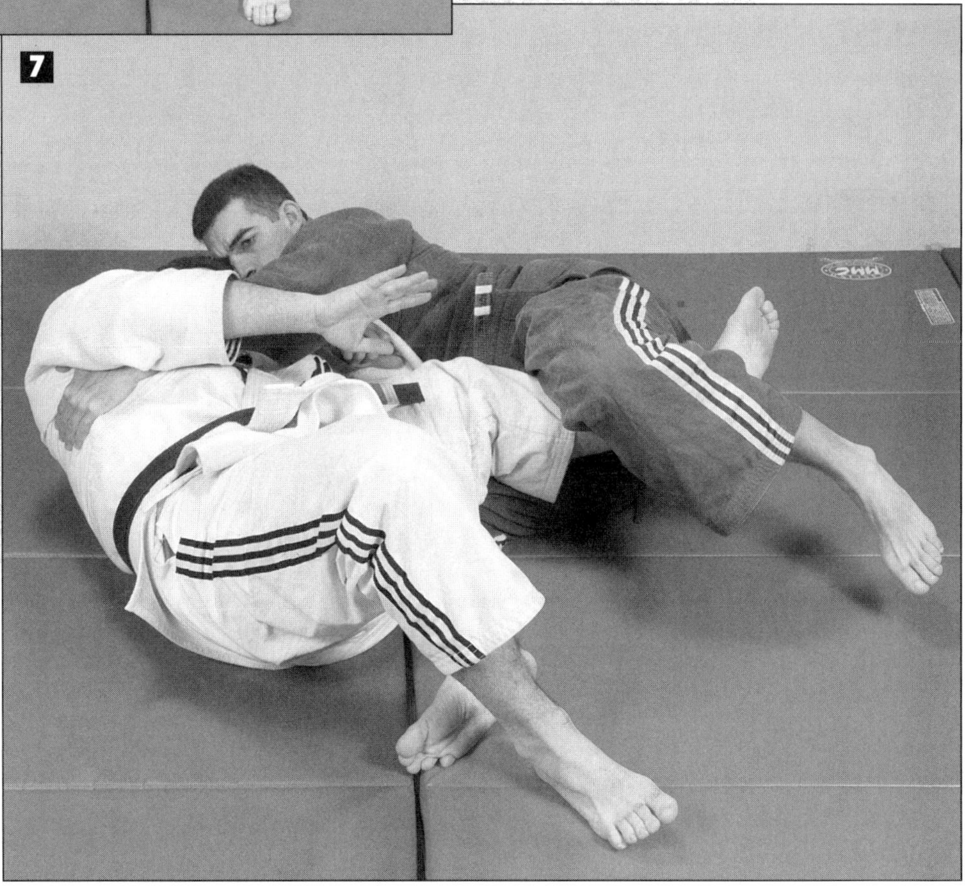

The opponent controls Rigan, who is on his hands and knees (1). Rigan moves his left leg to the outside and grabs the opponent's right leg with his left arm (2). This disrupts the opponent's balance and creates space for Rigan to move his right leg between the adversary's legs (3). He slides his hips forward and lifts his left leg over the opponent's right leg (4).

Escapes From The Back 13

By hooking his feet and moving his body to the side (5), Rigan forces the opponent into his half-guard (6). Now he can initiate the offensive.

The opponent controls Rigan (1), who moves away (2) while keeping his hands and feet on the ground (3). As he steps forward, Rigan grabs the opponent's right leg (4). Rigan sits (5),

Escapes From The Back 14

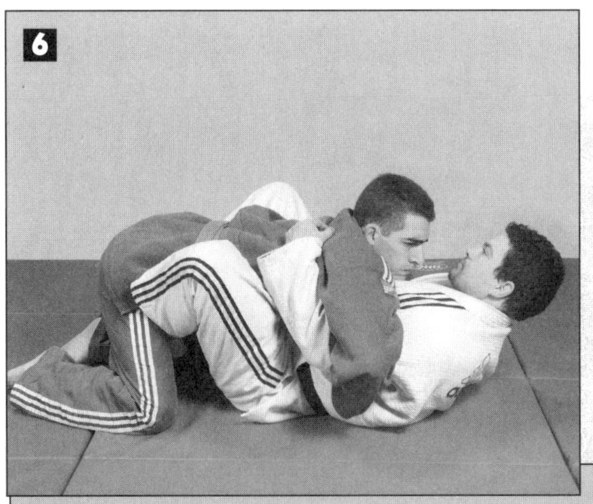

leans back (6) and brings his opponent inside his closed guard (7).

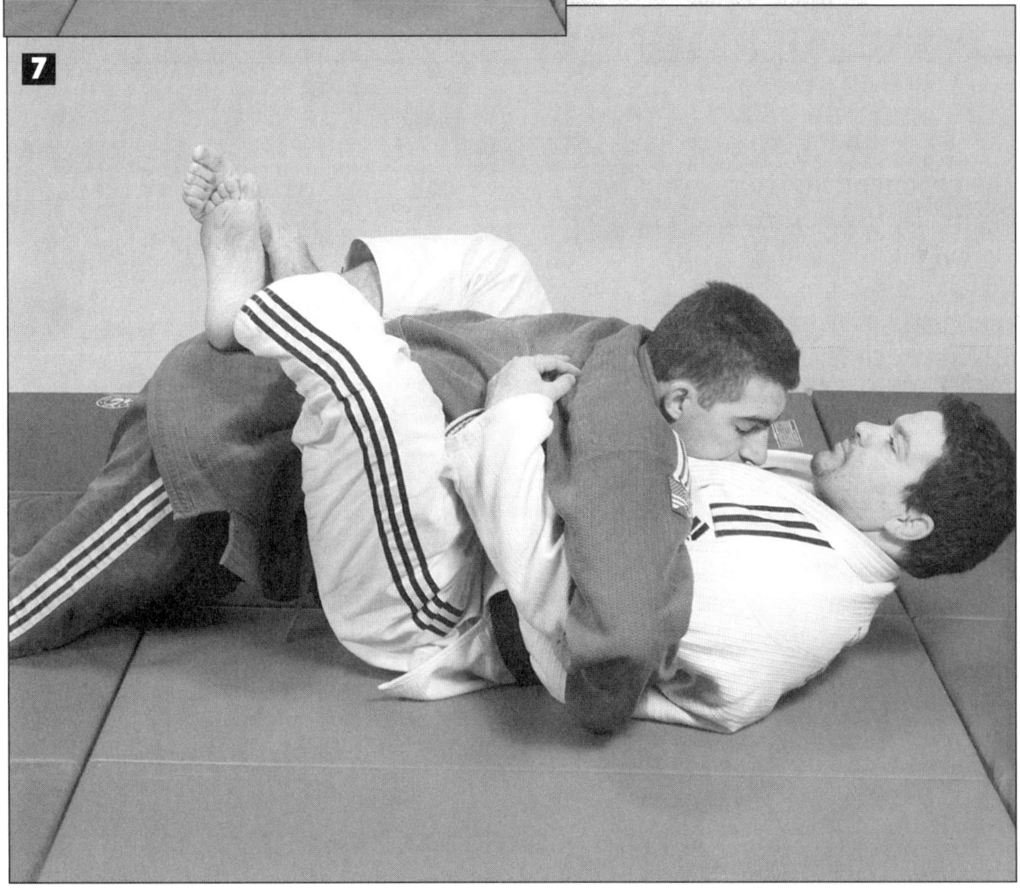

The opponent controls Rigan (1). Rigan shoots his left leg to the outside as he secures the opponent's right arm (2). Rigan slides his right leg forward (3),

Escapes From The Back 15

and immediately moves his hips to the other side; this forces the opponent's face into the floor (4). Rigan establishes control and applies a straight armlock (5).

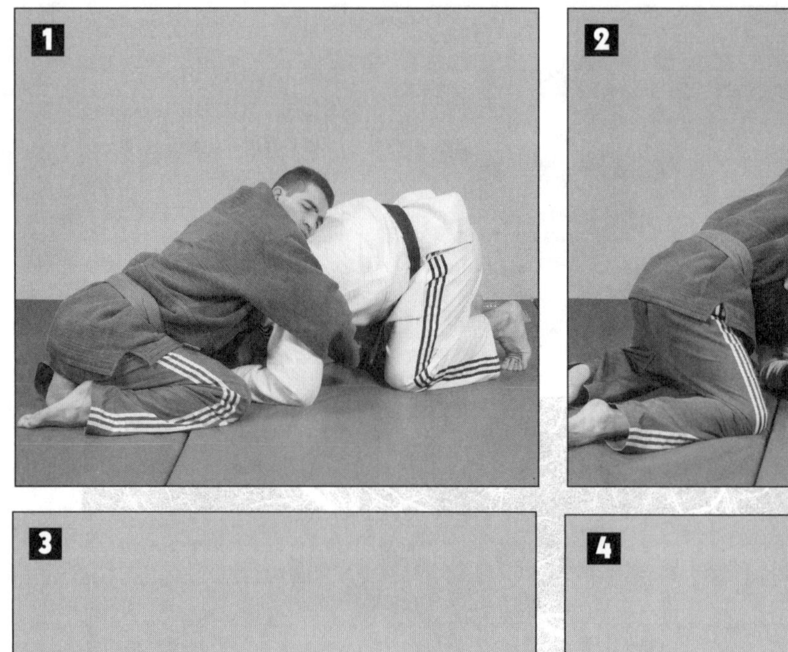

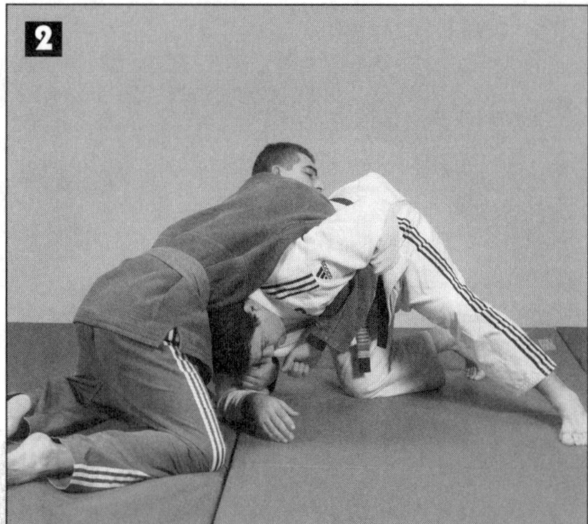

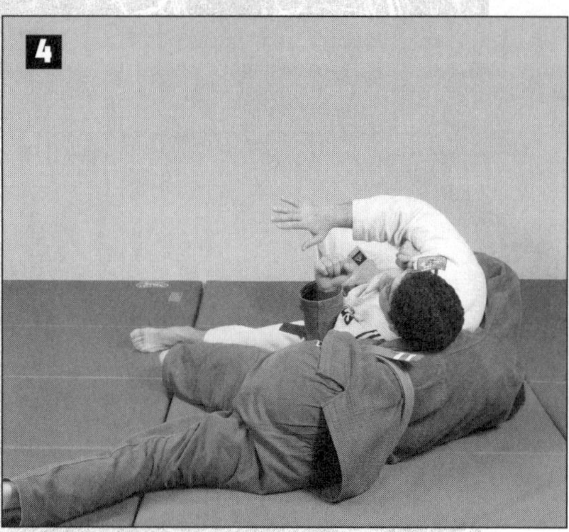

The opponent again establishes early control (1). Rigan grabs the opponent's right arm as he raises his hips to create space between himself and his adversary (2). He leans to the left and rolls, unbalancing the opponent and breaking the advantageous position (3).

Escapes From The Back 16

Rigan begins to roll to the other side (4). This gives him the proper position (5) to apply side control (6).

The opponent is on Rigan's back (1). Using his right hand, Rigan grabs the opponent's head. Then Rigan raises his hips (2) and forces the opponent forward as he rolls (3).

Escapes From The Back 17

This brings the opponent onto his back (4) and enables Rigan to apply full side control (5).

Rigan is under the opponent's control (1), so he uses both hands and feet to raise his hips (2). Using the space created by his previous movement, Rigan moves his head under the opponent's armpit and reaches for the adversary's right leg (3). Using his arm as support, Rigan moves his left leg to the side, raises his left arm (4),

Escapes From The Back 18

reaches around to the other side and moves to the opponent's back (5). He secures the position by controlling the opponent with both arms (6).

Attacks From The Mount

Vol. 3

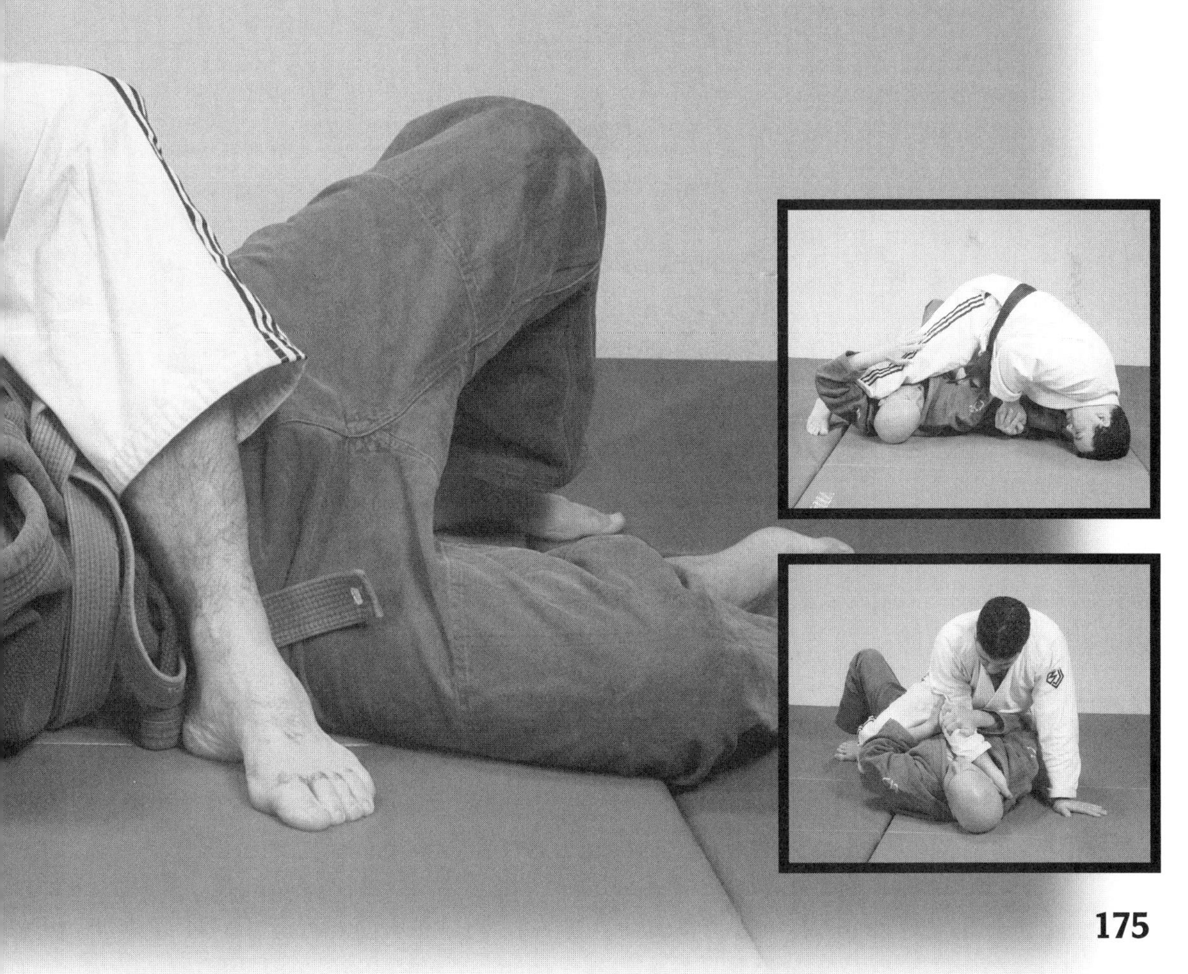

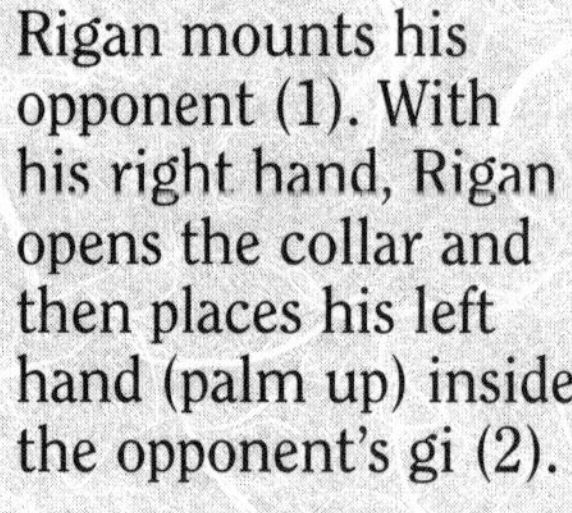

Rigan mounts his opponent (1). With his right hand, Rigan opens the collar and then places his left hand (palm up) inside the opponent's gi (2).

Attacks From The Mount 1

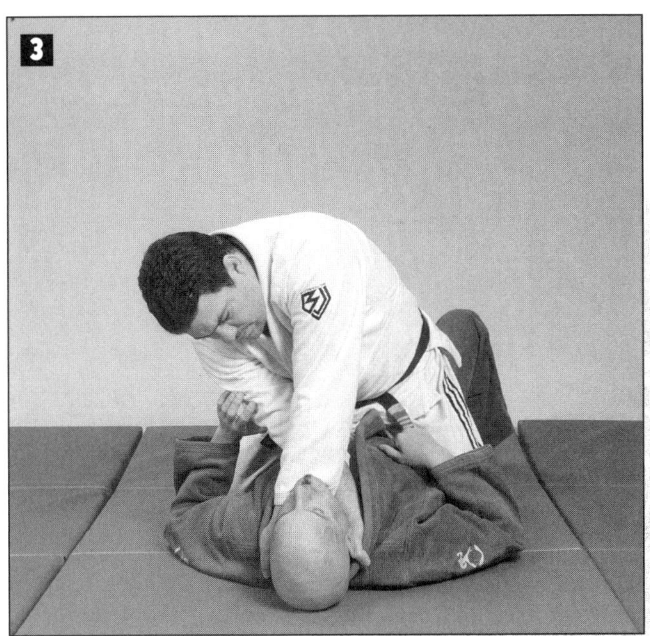

He slides his right hand under his left until both hands touch at the back of the opponent's neck (3). Leaning forward, Rigan applies pressure and executes the choke (4).

Rigan mounts his opponent (1). While he opens the collar with his right hand, Rigan places his left hand (palm up) inside the opponent's gi (2). Using his right hand (palm down) (3),

Attacks From The Mount 2

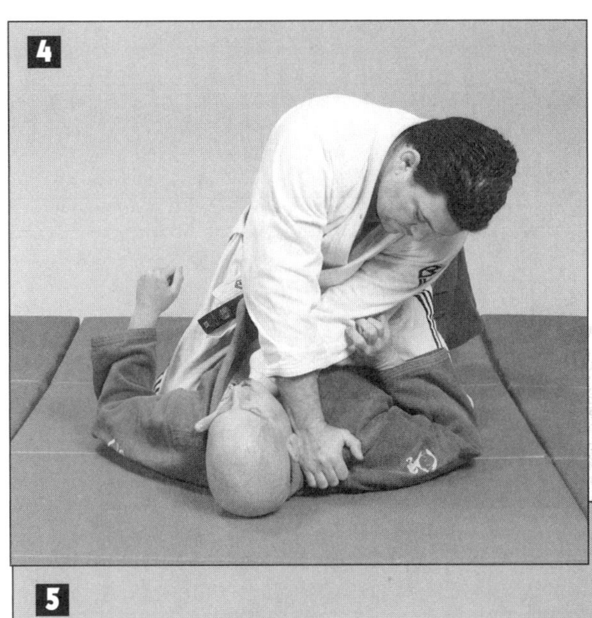

Rigan grabs the right side of the opponent's collar (4). Leaning forward, Rigan applies pressure and chokes his opponent out (5).

While mounting his opponent, Rigan grabs the left side of the collar (1). Again, the palm is down. Then he grabs (palm down) the other side of the collar with his left hand (2).

Attacks From The Mount 3

To choke his opponent, he brings both hands together (3).

3

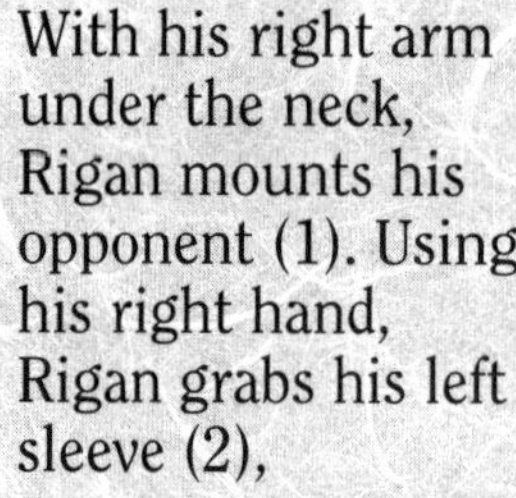

With his right arm under the neck, Rigan mounts his opponent (1). Using his right hand, Rigan grabs his left sleeve (2),

and then raises his left arm adjacent to his opponent's neck (3). He places his arm across the opponent's neck, exerts pressure and chokes him with an *ezequiel* (4).

While mounting his adversary, Rigan adjusts his left leg as soon as he feels him turning to the right (1). With his left hand, Rigan opens the opponent's gi (2).

Attacks From The Mount 5

He uses his right hand to grab the opponent's collar (3). To apply a finishing choke, he pulls with his right hand and crosses his left arm over the opponent's neck (4).

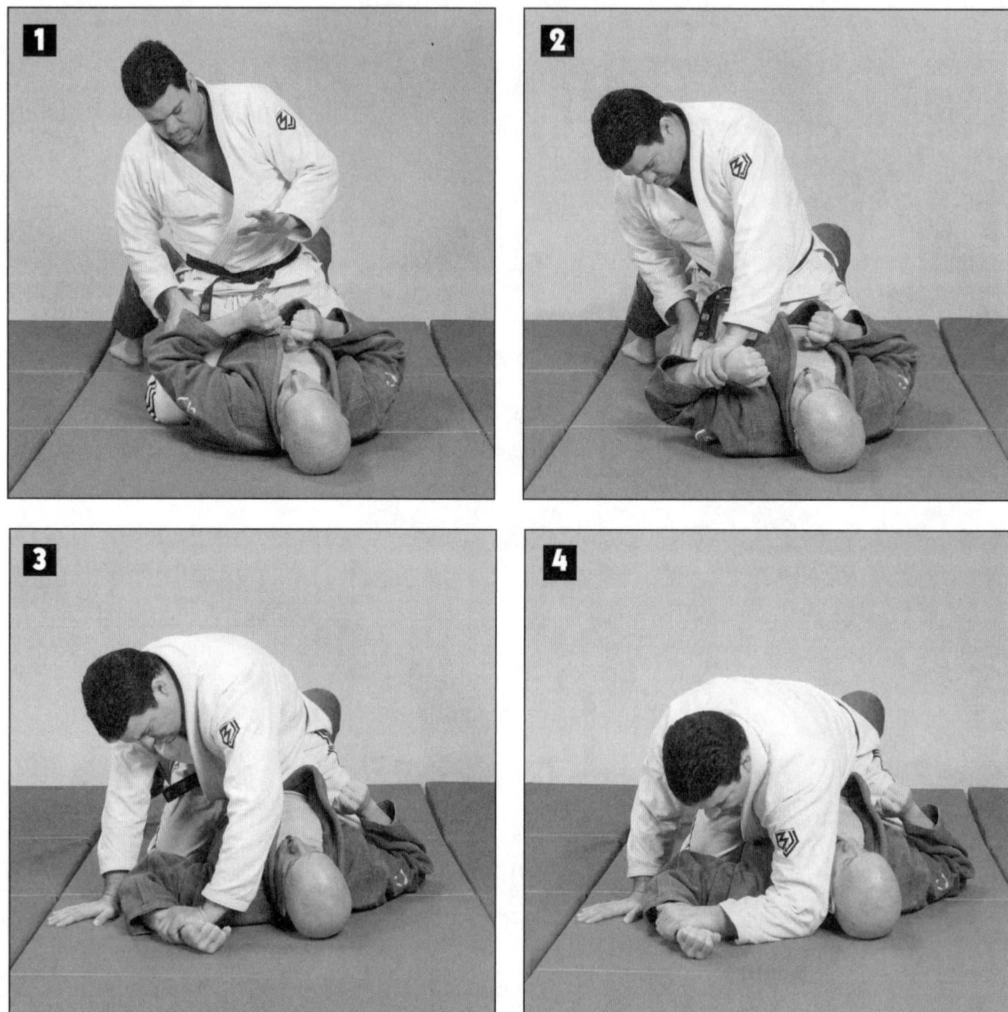

Rigan mounts his opponent (1). With his left hand, he grabs the opponent's left wrist (2) and forces it to the ground (3). Rigan uses his elbow to establish position (4), as he moves his right hand under the opponent's left arm so he can

Attacks From The Mount 6

grab his own wrist (5). By lifting the adversary's right arm, Rigan creates pressure and applies a bent armlock (6).

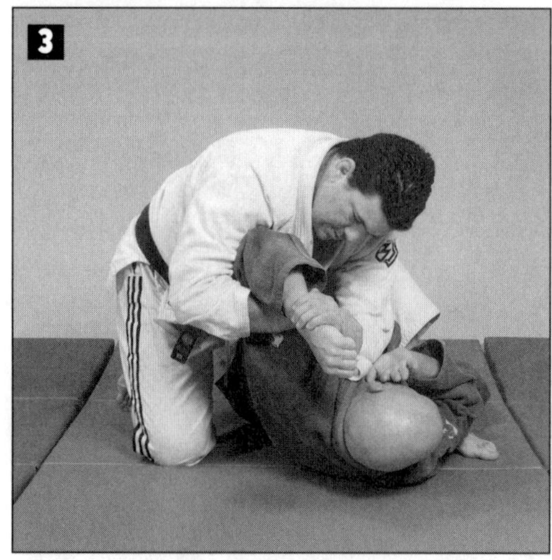

As Rigan mounts his opponent, he tries to apply the previous technique (1), but the opponent turns to the right to avoid the pressure (2). In response, Rigan adjusts his position and lifts his left knee (3). Notice that he hasn't released his grip. As the opponent keeps turning, Rigan follows him (4).

Attacks From The Mount 7

Rigan sits and passes his right leg over the opponent (5). He leans back and applies a finishing armlock (6).

Rigan mounts his opponent, who tries to push him away with his right hand (1). Rigan uses both hands to establish his position (2), and then he adjusts his hips as he turns to the right (3).

Notice that he maintains the pressure on the opponent's chest. He moves his left leg toward the opponent's head (4), places both legs across the opponent, sits back and applies a straight armlock (5).

Rigan controls his opponent from the mounted position (1). As soon as the opponent attempts to push Rigan's left knee away so he can escape, Rigan grabs the wrist (2) and establishes position with his right arm (3).

Attacks From The Mount

Rigan wraps his right arm under the opponent's right arm, grabs his own wrist (4) and applies a *kimura* (5).

Rigan mounts his opponent with his right hand inside the collar (1). Rigan switches his hip position, places his left elbow close to the opponent's neck, applies pressure (2),

leans forward and chokes him (3).

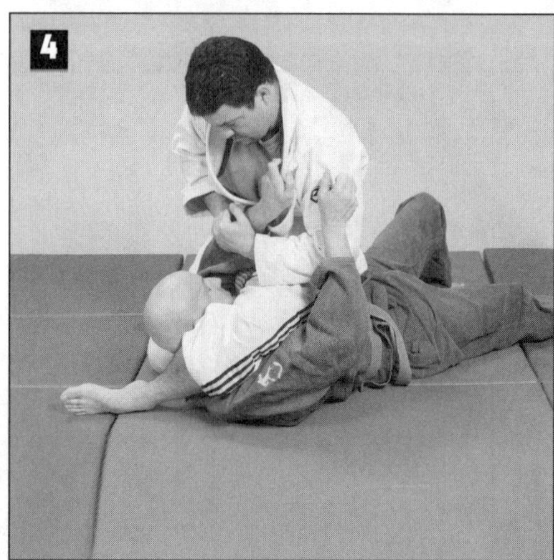

Rigan controls the altercation from the mounted position with his right arm under the opponent's head (1). With his left hand, Rigan grabs the opponent's right wrist (2). He places his left leg between the opponent's head and his extended left arm and then grabs his ankle to secure the position (3). He switches grips and pulls the opponent's right arm as he slides his left leg behind the head (4).

Attacks From The Mount 11

Moving his right leg forward so he can hook the instep of his left foot under his right leg (5), Rigan secures the position and applies a *triangle* choke from the top (6).

Rigan controls the opponent from the mounted position (1). Notice that his left arm is under the adversary's right arm. Securing his position with his left arm, Rigan slides forward and moves his right knee over the opponent's left arm (2). This creates additional pressure (3), so he can extend his body and execute the straight armbar (4).

Attacks From The Mount 12

Note: It is important to maintain pressure and control on the opponent's right arm during the entire movement. Keep it tight. If necessary, grab your own gi to secure the control.

Rigan controls the opponent from a half-mounted position (1). With his left hand, he loosens the opponent's gi (2). He traps the opponent's right arm by grabbing the tip of the gi with his right hand (3). He leans back and maintains the grip with his right hand (4).

Attacks From The Mount 13

Rigan releases the gi as he moves his right leg around the opponent's neck and under his left leg (5). He leans back and secures the straight armlock (6).

Rigan controls the opponent from the half-mount (1). Notice that he has both of the opponent's arms. He leans back (2), releases the grip of his right hand (3),

Attacks From The Mount 14

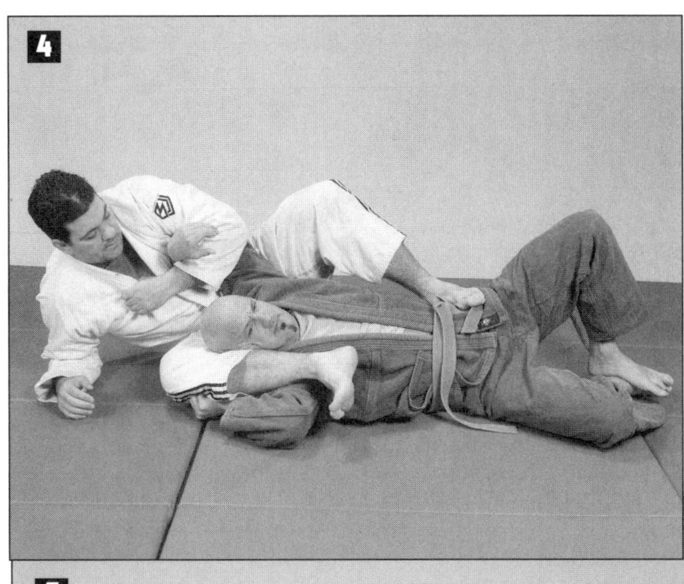

and slides to the side so he can get the right angle (4) to execute a reverse *triangle* choke from the back (5).

While controlling the confrontation from the half-mount, Rigan grabs the opponent's left hand (1). Rigan then pushes the opponent's arm toward the ground (2). Using his right hand, Rigan reaches around the neck and grabs the adversary's left wrist (3). To establish a better and tighter position, Rigan pushes the opponent's left elbow (4).

Attacks From The Mount 15

He slides his hand to the opponent's left wrist, turns and ends up completely on his opponent's back (5-6). From here, Rigan can apply a finishing choke (7).

Rigan grabs the opponent's left hand and controls him from the half-mounted position (1). He forces the opponent's left hand to the side so he can grab it with his right hand (2). Then he pushes the opponent's left elbow to get a better and tighter position (3). Rigan sits up, adopts the back position (4),

slides his arm across the opponent's neck (5), leans back, cranks on the collar and chokes him (6).

Rigan controls his opponent from the mounted position (1). To create room to move his left leg forward, Rigan pulls his opponent's sleeves (2).

Attacks From The Mount 17

While maintaining the grip with his right hand, Rigan leans back and grabs his opponent's left leg (3). From there, Rigan applies a straight armlock on his opponent's left arm (4).

Rigan mounts his opponent (1). Notice that his right arm is firmly around the adversary's neck. Using his left hand, Rigan pushes the opponent's right arm across the chest (2). To establish position, Rigan leans forward and clutches his wrists (3).

Attacks From The Mount 18

He starts to move his right leg to the other side. Once it reaches the opponent's right hip, he'll have better control (4). To submit his opponent, he extends his left leg and applies a choke (5).

With his right hand inside the collar, Rigan controls the opponent from the mounted position (1). Using his left hand, Rigan pushes the opponent to the right (2). This enables Rigan to establish his balance (3), so he can put his left knee close to the opponent's head without losing equilibrium and control (4-5).

Attacks From The Mount 19

Using his left hand for support, Rigan places his left leg over the opponent's head (6-7), leans back and executes a straight armlock (8).

While firmly grabbing the collar, Rigan mounts his opponent (1). Rigan then sets his right leg close to the opponent's head (2-3). As soon as he feels the opponent's left hand pushing, Rigan releases the grip (4), switches hip position (5),

Attacks From The Mount 20

and goes to side control (6). Here he can apply a choke (7).

Rigan mounts his opponent (1). Attempting to escape, the opponent uses both hands to push Rigan (2). Rigan takes advantage of the action and allows his body to move to the side (3).

Attacks From The Mount 21

He places his left leg under the opponent's head (4), turns to the side and applies a straight armlock (5).

Escapes From The Mount

Vol. 3

The opponent controls Rigan from the mounted position (1). Using both hands, Rigan reaches around and grabs the opponent's belt (2). To create leverage, he puts his left foot between the belt and the opponent's back (3-4). As Rigan pushes, he simultaneously places his hands on the opponent's hips (5)

Escapes From The Mount 1

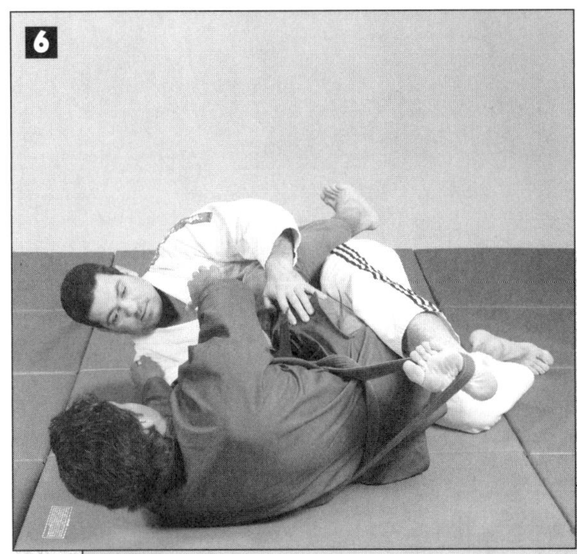

so he can sweep him to the right (6). Rigan ends up inside the opponent's guard (7).

The opponent mounts Rigan (1). Taking advantage of the opponent's raised left knee, Rigan underhooks the leg with his right hand (2), pushes with his right arm and simultaneously "bridges" to get momentum (3) so he can push the opponent away from his chest (4).

Escapes From The Mount 2

While holding the opponent's left leg, Rigan starts to turn (5) so he can initiate the counterattack (6).

The adversary controls Rigan from the mounted position (1). Rigan grabs the opponent's pants with his right hand (2) and "bridges" as he pulls the leg up (3). This creates space for Rigan to move his left leg under the opponent's leg (4).

Escapes From The Mount 3

He uses his right foot to push the opponent's left leg away (5-6). When the adversary hits the ground (7), Rigan can escape (8).

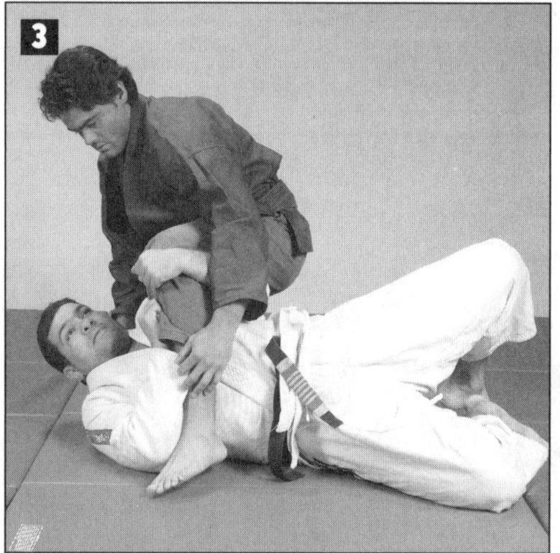

Using the mount, the opponent controls Rigan (1). As Rigan passes his left arm under the opponent's left leg and latches on, he simultaneously grabs the pants with his right hand (2). Using these grips as support, Rigan "bridges" (3) and turns to the side to escape (4).

He is now behind the opponent (5), and he can initiate the offense (6).

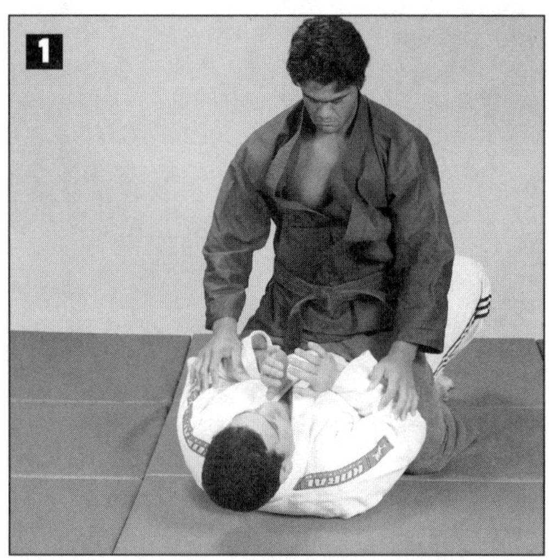

Employing the mount, the opponent controls Rigan (1). Utilizing his elbows to keep the opponent's knees away from his armpits, Rigan moves his hips to the right as he pushes the opponent's left knee away (2). This enables him to plant his right foot behind the opponent's left leg (3). To create space, Rigan moves his hips to the right (4) as he pushes the opponent's right

knee away (5). He wraps his left leg around the opponent and closes the guard (6).

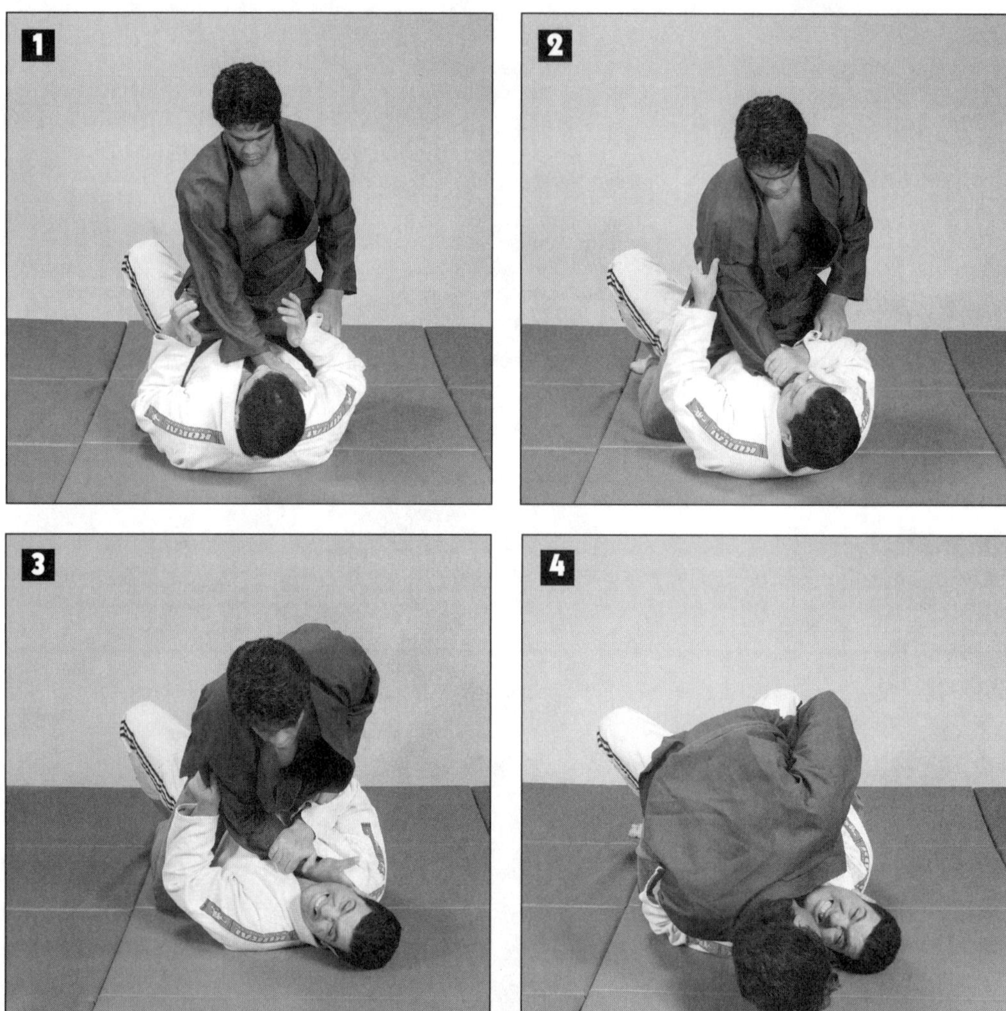

The opponent mounts Rigan and places his right hand inside the collar (1). Using his right hand, Rigan controls the opponent's right hand. With his left, he secures the opponent's right elbow (2). Then he "bridges" to the left (3), which throws the opponent onto the ground (4-5).

Escapes From The Mount 6

Rigan continues to roll until he is in the opponent's closed guard (6).

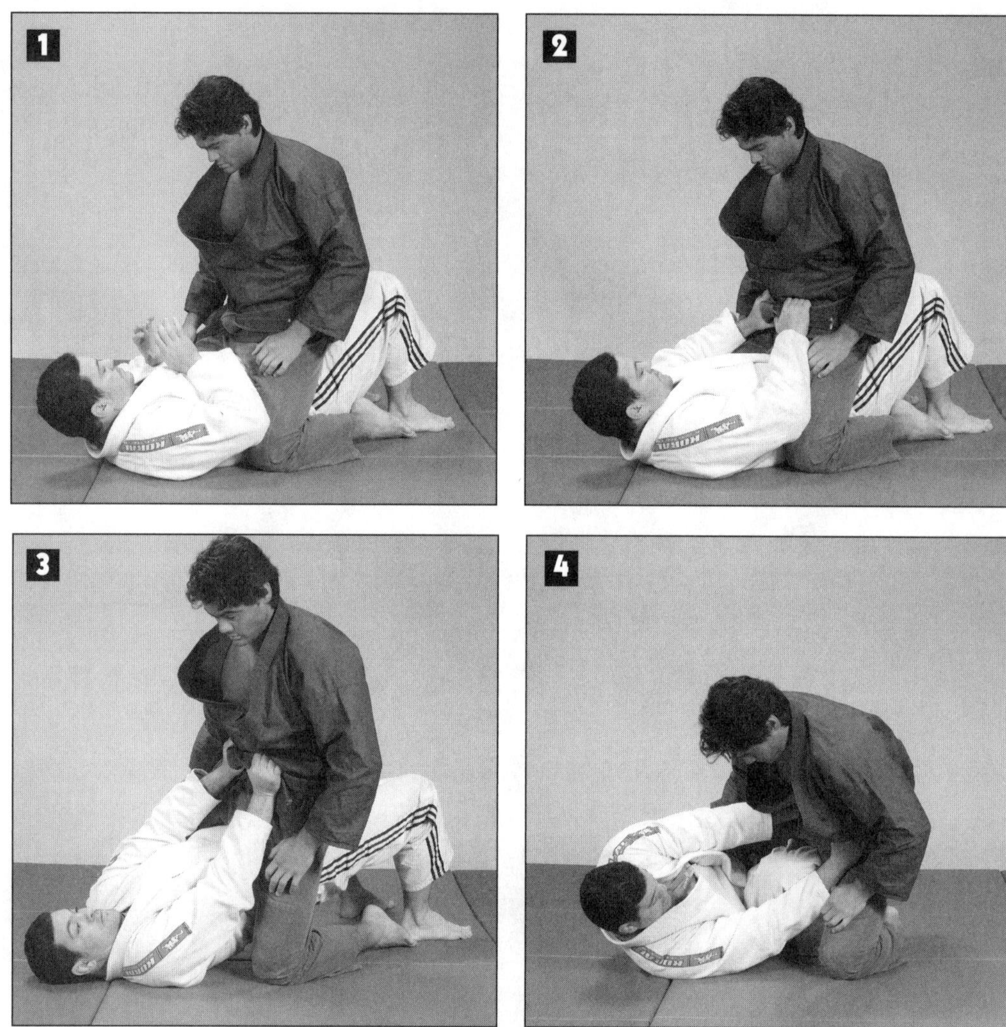

The opponent controls Rigan from the mounted position (1). Rigan grabs the opponent's belt with both hands (2) and pushes up as he "bridges" to create some space (3). This enables him to bring his right knee toward his chest (4),

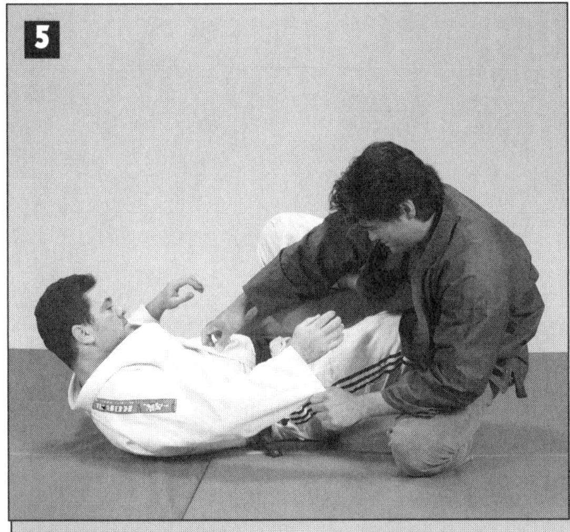

place his foot on the opponent and push him away (5). When the adversary hits the ground, Rigan applies an anklelock (6).

The opponent mounts Rigan (1). To create space, Rigan "bridges" and pushes the opponent away (2). He raises both legs (3), places them in the opponent's armpits and pushes (4). Rigan quickly moves to his hands and knees and grabs the opponent's right foot (5).

He circles his right arm around the opponent's foot (6) and applies a footlock (7).

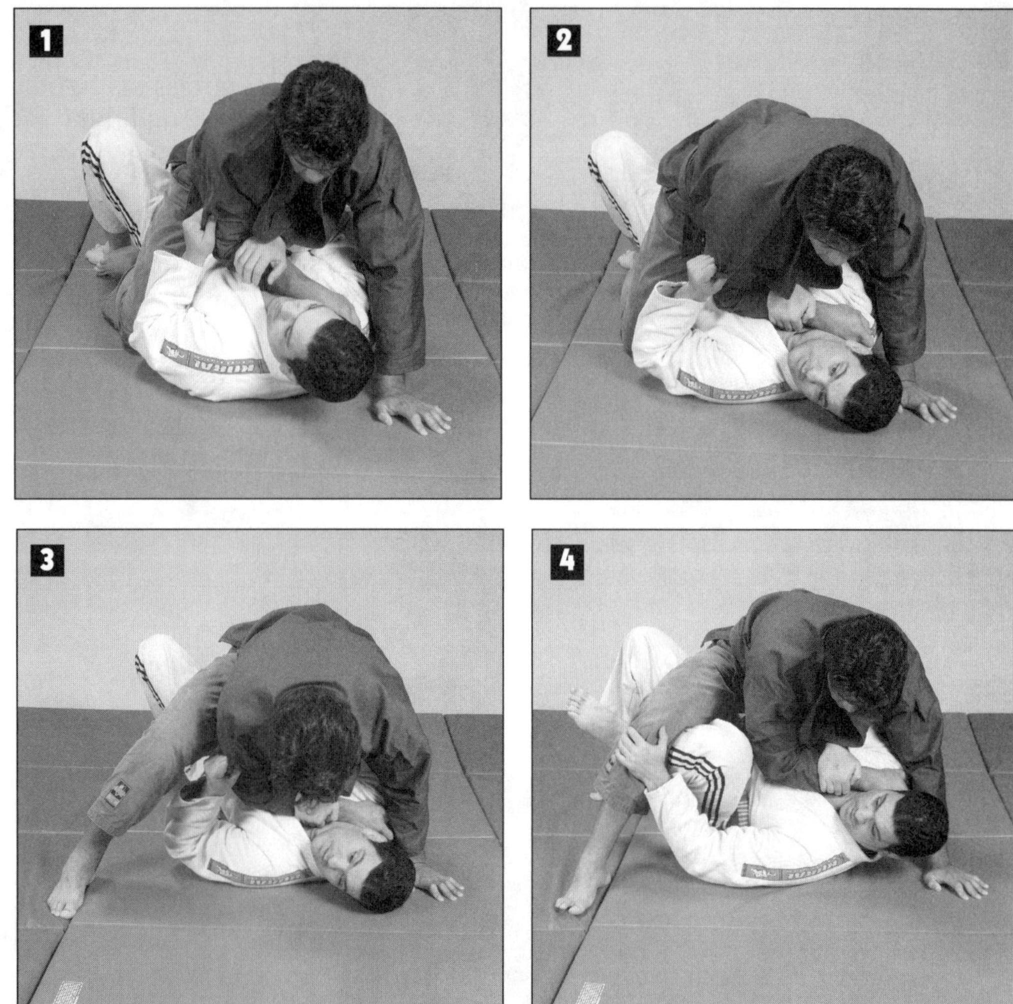

Mounted by the opponent (1), Rigan tries to escape using the "bridge" (2). However, the opponent shoots his right leg to the outside and blocks Rigan's attempt (3). In response, Rigan moves his left knee towards his chest (4).

Escapes From The Mount 

Now he can either sweep the opponent (5) or bring him into his half-guard (6).

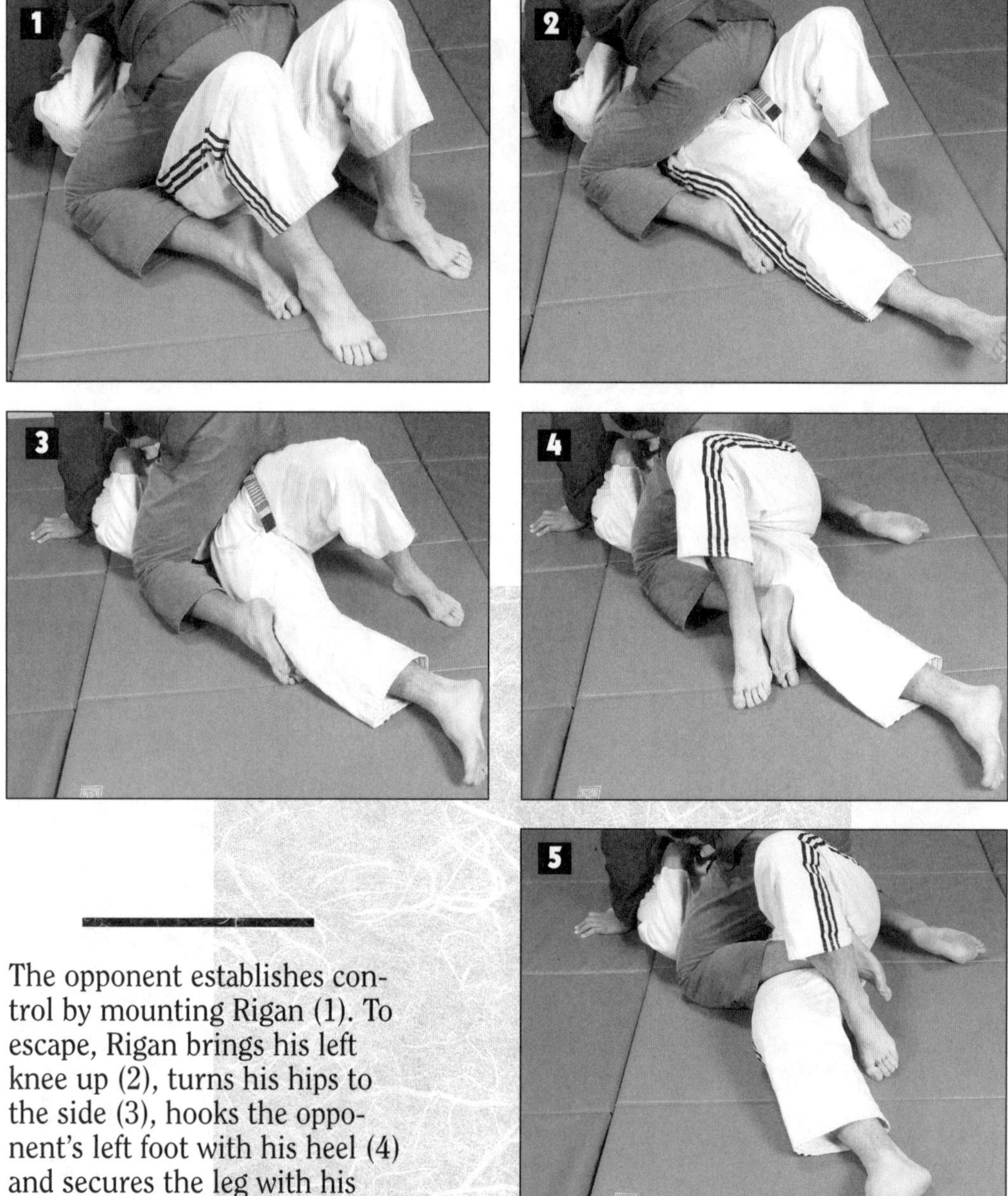

The opponent establishes control by mounting Rigan (1). To escape, Rigan brings his left knee up (2), turns his hips to the side (3), hooks the opponent's left foot with his heel (4) and secures the leg with his right leg (5).

Escapes From The Mount 10

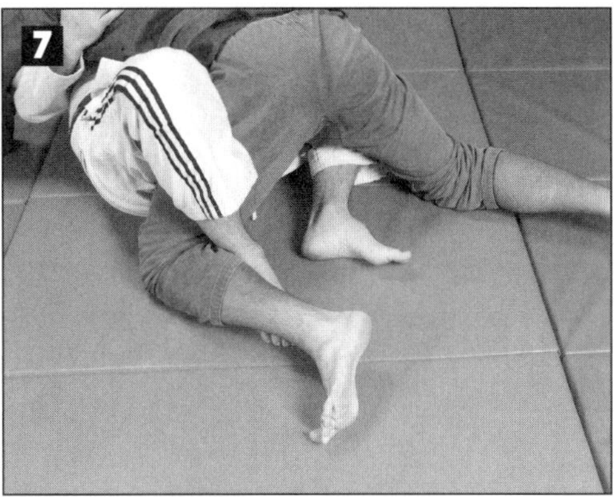

Rigan slides his hips to the other side and extricates his right knee (6). He hooks the opponent's left leg with his right foot as he starts to move his left knee outside (7). Finally, he adopts the closed guard (8).

1
2
3
4
5
6

Escapes From The Mount 11

The opponent mounts Rigan (1). To create space, Rigan brings his left knee up (2) and turns his hips to the side (3) so he can hook the opponent's left foot (4). Rigan brings the foot over his right leg and secures it with his left heel (5-6). As he controls the opponent's left leg with his left foot (7), Rigan slides his hips to the outside (8) so he can extricate his left leg. Wrapping both legs around the opponent, Rigan puts him in his closed guard (9).

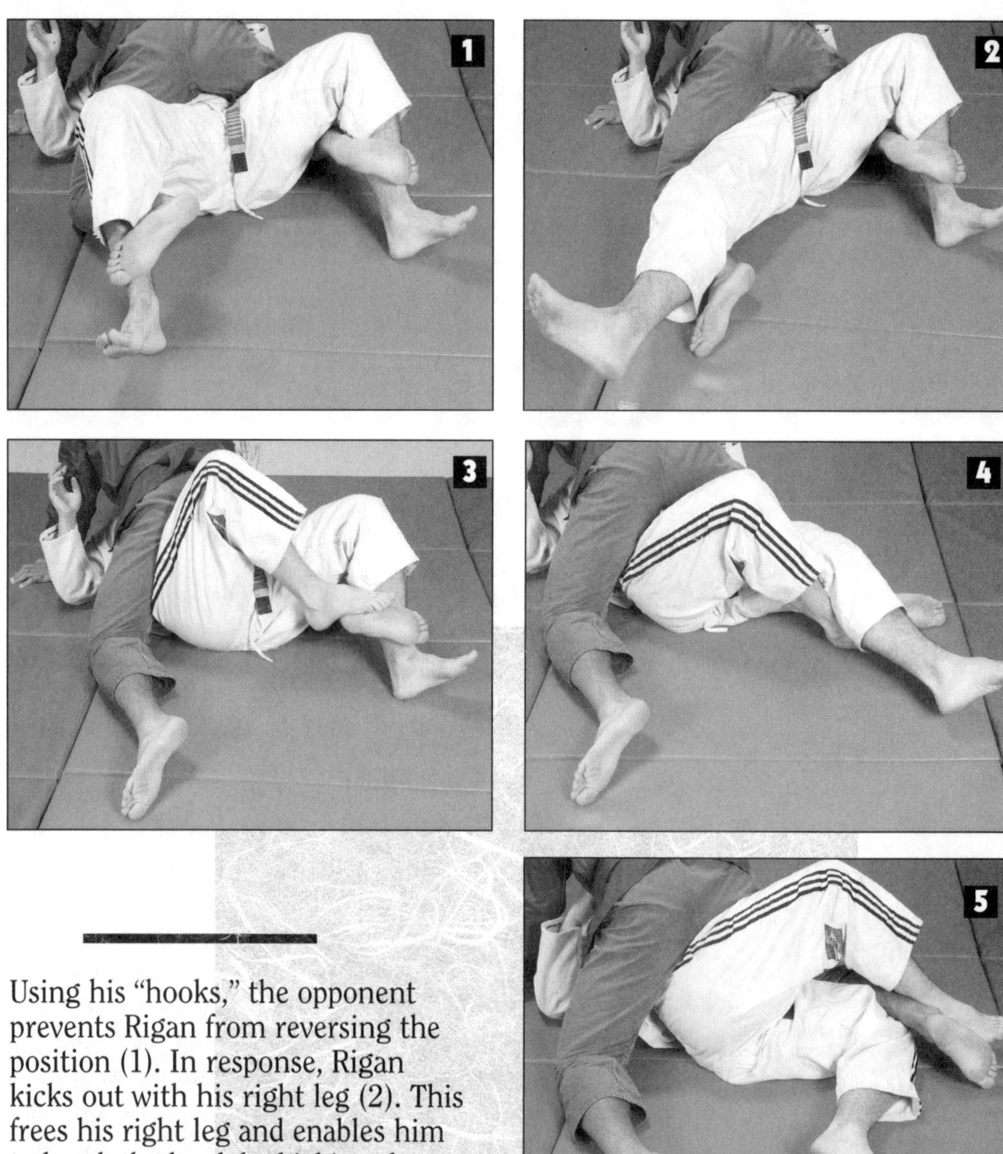

Using his "hooks," the opponent prevents Rigan from reversing the position (1). In response, Rigan kicks out with his right leg (2). This frees his right leg and enables him to break the hook by kicking the opponent's right foot (3-4). Rigan turns his hips on an angle (5)

Escapes From The Mount 12

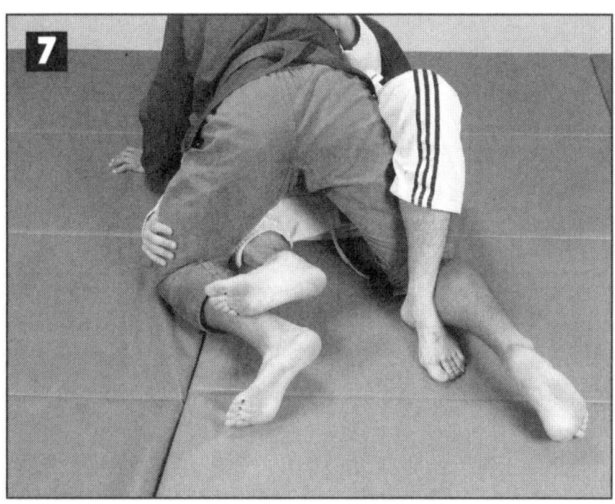

as he shifts his left leg to the outside (6). Notice that he is controlling the opponent's right leg with his right leg. While Rigan now uses his left foot to control the opponent's right leg, he pushes the opponent's left thigh (7). This gives him space to extricate his right knee, and he pulls his opponent into the closed guard (8).

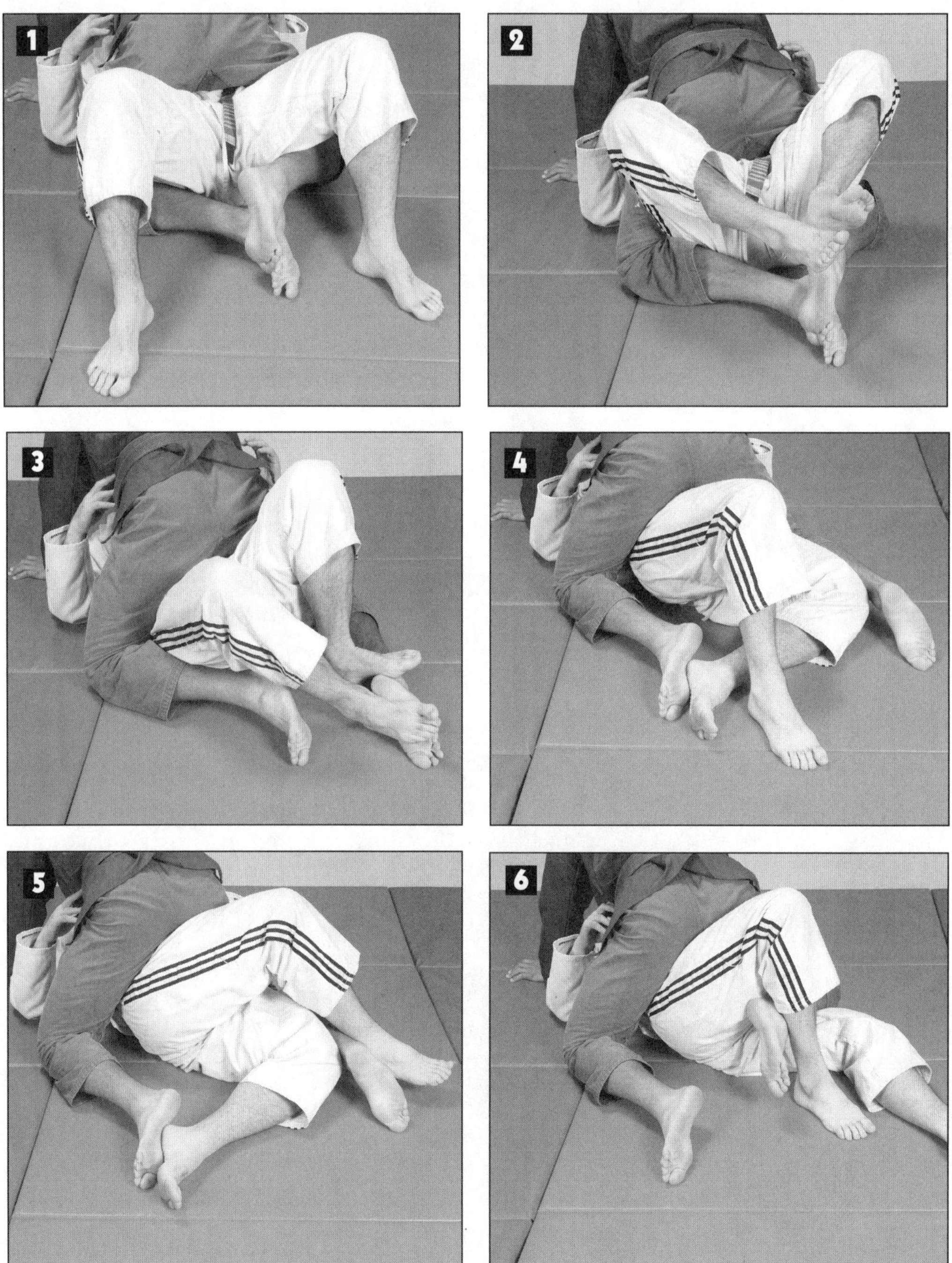
1
2
3
4
5
6

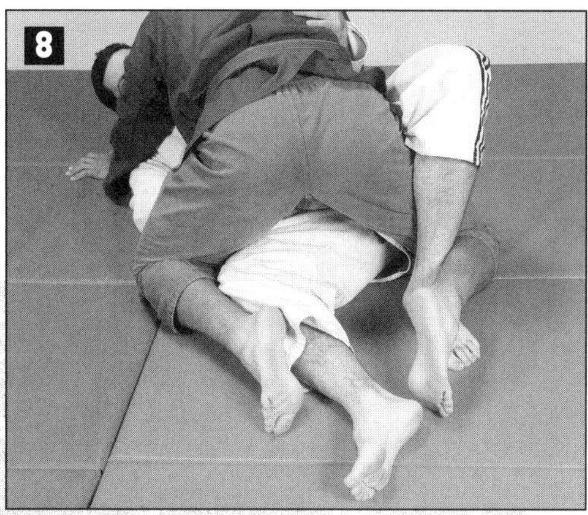

The opponent hooks both feet close to Rigan's buttocks. This prevents Rigan from using "footwork" to reverse the position (1). To create momentum and space, Rigan raises both legs (2), breaks the "hooks" and pushes the opponent's right leg away (3). Rigan twists his hips (4) and traps the opponent's right foot (5) between his legs (6). During this maneuver, Rigan maintains control of the foot with his right foot. Once he has established this position (7), Rigan slides his hips to the other side (8), moves his right leg outside and pulls the opponent into his closed guard (9).

1

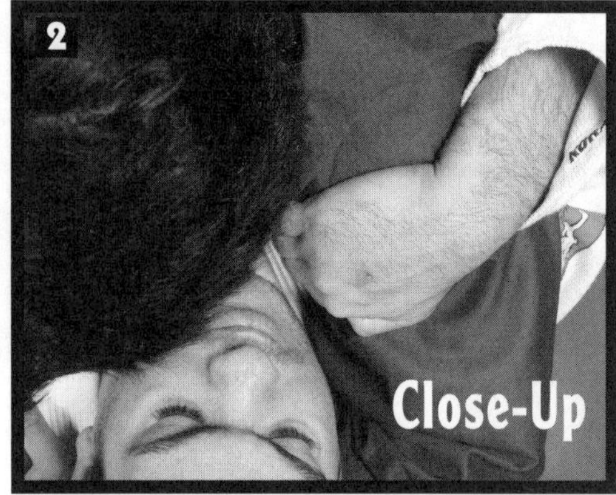
2

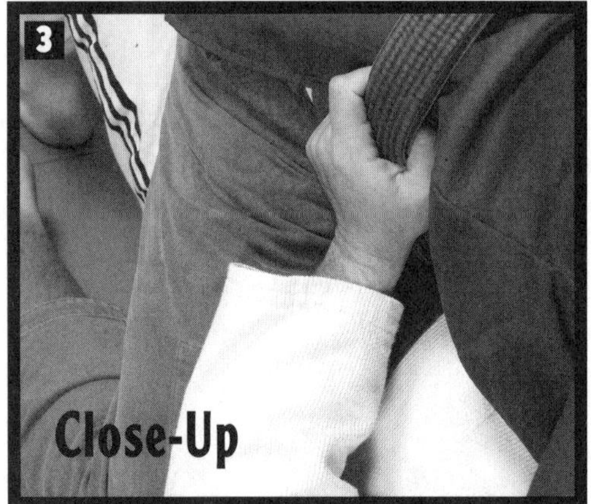
3

4

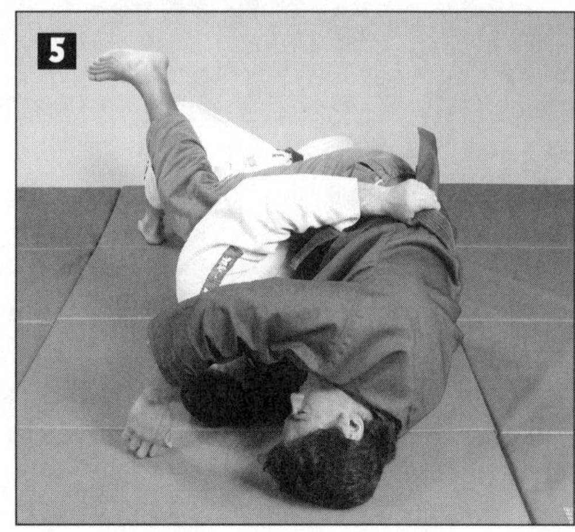
5

The opponent mounts Rigan (1). In response, Rigan secures the opponent's left arm. This is a close-up (2). Using his left hand, Rigan grabs the opponent's belt (3). To support himself when he "bridges" and to prevent the opponent from breaking the grip, Rigan moves his head to the ground (4) and then sweeps him to the right (5).

Escapes From The Mount 14

Rigan rolls with him (6) and ends up inside his closed guard (7).

While supporting himself with his hands, the opponent controls Rigan (1). Using his right arm, Rigan hooks the opponent's left arm (2), and he secures the grip with his left hand (3). He pulls the opponent's arm down (4) to keep it close to his body (5).

Escapes From The Mount 15

Despite the opponent's attempt to stop him, Rigan executes a "bridge" (6). The opponent falls to his side (7). Rigan ultimately ends up in his opponent's closed guard (8), where he can initiate the offensive response.

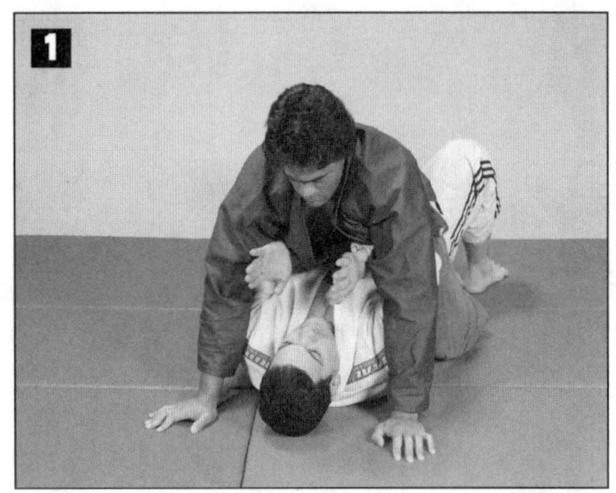

Using his hands for support, the opponent mounts Rigan (1). Rigan wraps his arms around the opponent (2-4) and secures the position by grabbing the belt with both hands (5).

Escapes From The Mount 16

He “bridges,” turns to the right (6) and roles the opponent to the side (7). He can now initiate the offense from inside the closed guard (8).

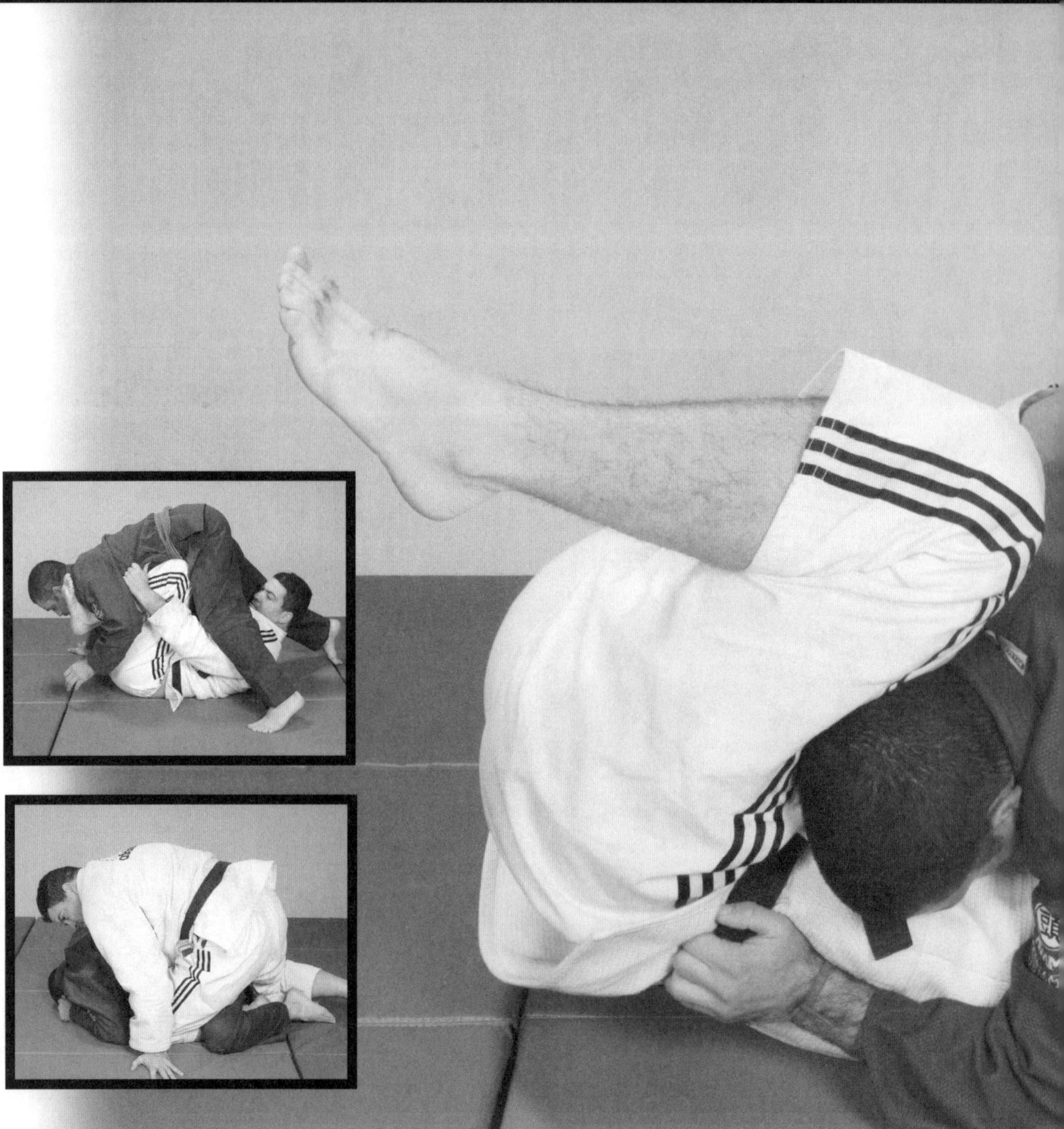

North & South

Vol. 3

The fighters are in the north-south position, and Rigan is on the bottom (1). Employing his left hand, Rigan grabs the opponent's belt (2). Then he slides slightly away, reaches up and grabs his right foot (3-4).

North & South 1

He traps the opponent's belt with his right foot (5),

continued

continued from page 255

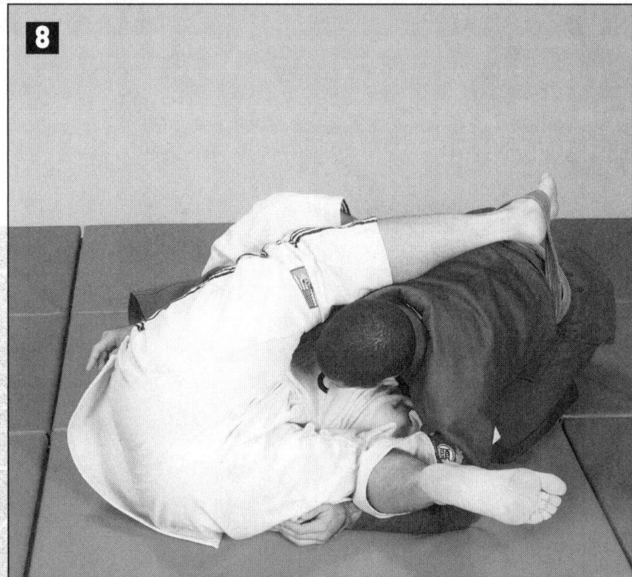

and uses it as support (6) to move away (7). Rigan slides his head out (8),

North & South 1

turns around (9) and puts the opponent inside his open guard (10).

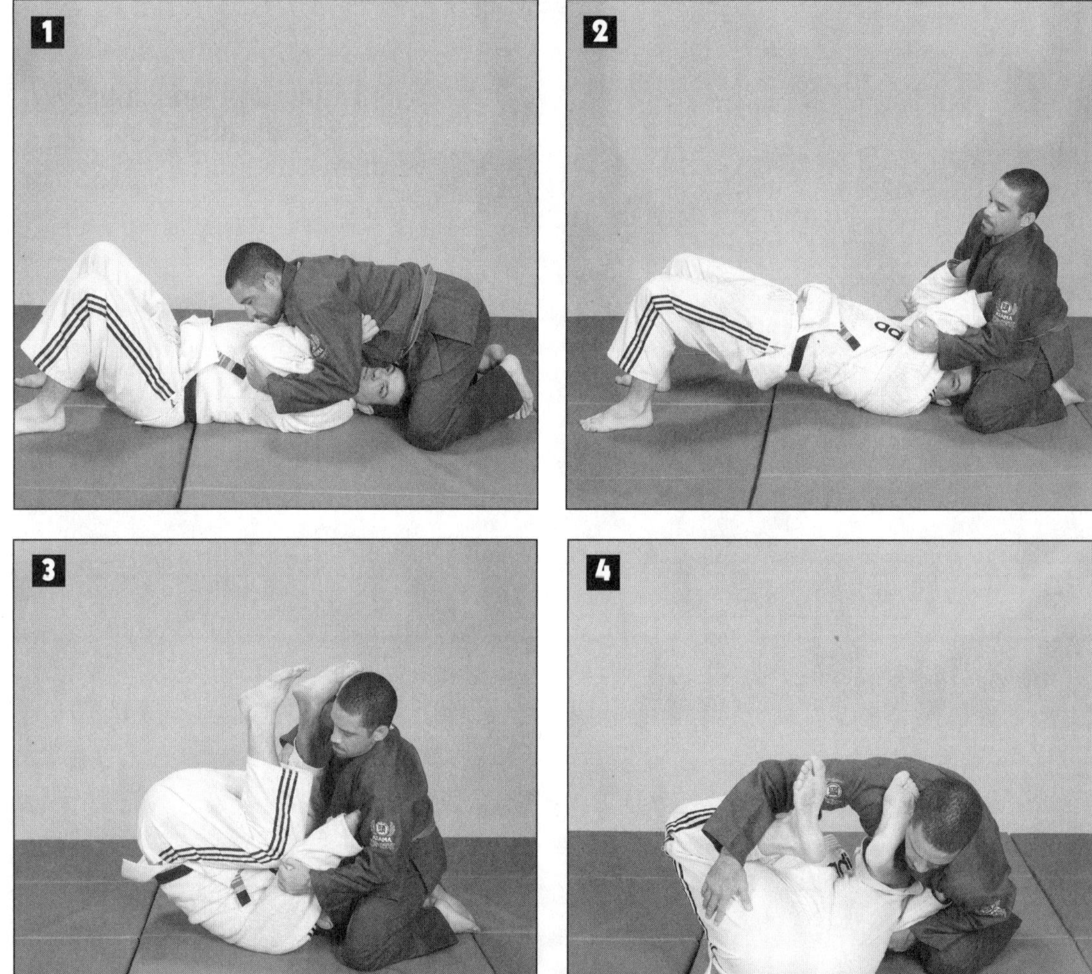

Rigan is again under the opponent's body (1). Rigan "bridges" and pushes the opponent away with both hands (2). Keeping his knees close to his body, Rigan raises his legs (3), pivots to the right (4),

North & South 2

and escapes (5). He can now put the opponent in the open guard (6).

The combatants are in the north-south position, and Rigan is on the bottom (1). Utilizing both hands, Rigan "bridges" and pushes the opponent away (2). He raises his legs, keeps his knees close to his body (3) and pulls the opponent forward (4). During this maneuver, Rigan controls the adversary with his legs (5-6).

North & South 3

While maintaining control, Rigan grabs the opponent's right leg (7) and applies a straight kneebar (8).

While in the north-south position, Rigan starts underneath (1). Rigan immediately "bridges" and pushes the opponent away (2). He lifts both legs, keeping his knees close to his body (3).

North & South 4

Then he puts his right foot under the opponent's right armpit (4), and his left in the left armpit (5).

continued

continued from page 263

By simultaneously pulling with his hands while pushing with his feet (6), Rigan disrupts the opponent's balance (7). The adversary ends up on the ground (8), where Rigan can initiate the offense (9)

from the side (10).

The fighters are in the north-south position, and Rigan is on the bottom (1). Using both hands while he "bridges," Rigan pushes the opponent away (2). Keeping his knees tight to his chest, Rigan raises his legs (3-4), and passes his right leg under the opponent's left armpit (5).

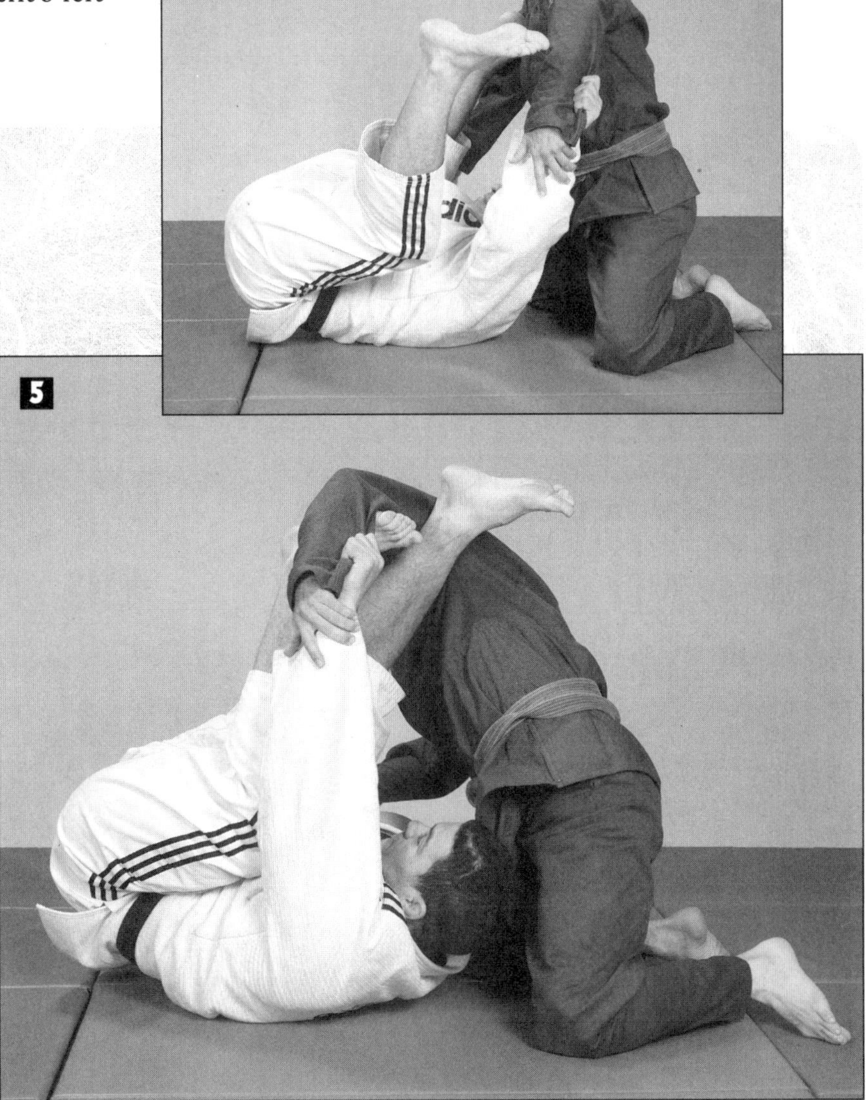

continued

continued from page 267

6

7

8

This gives him leverage to spin to the left (6), as he simultaneously pulls himself into the opponent's guard (7-8).

Rigan grabs his left foot with his right hand (9), and applies a *triangle* choke (10).

The fighters begin in the north-south position (1). Rigan again is underneath. Rigan "bridges" and pushes the opponent's hips away (2). By swinging his legs, Rigan generates momentum (3) to place his right leg under the opponent's left leg (4). Rigan immediately traps the leg by closing his legs (5).

North & South 6

While grabbing the opponent's belt, Rigan slides forward (6), moves to the opponent's left (7), and initiates the offense from the back (8).

Rigan is on the bottom as the fighters begin in the north-south position (1). He grabs the opponent's left leg (2) and secures the hold with his right hand (3). This provides leverage to prevent the opponent from standing (4).

Once he controls the opponent's body, Rigan moves his knees closer (5), slides his body and head under the opponent, and

continued

continued from page 273

throws him (6-8) to the right (9).

North & South 7

Rigan controls the opponent's legs (10), and initiates the attack from the side (11).

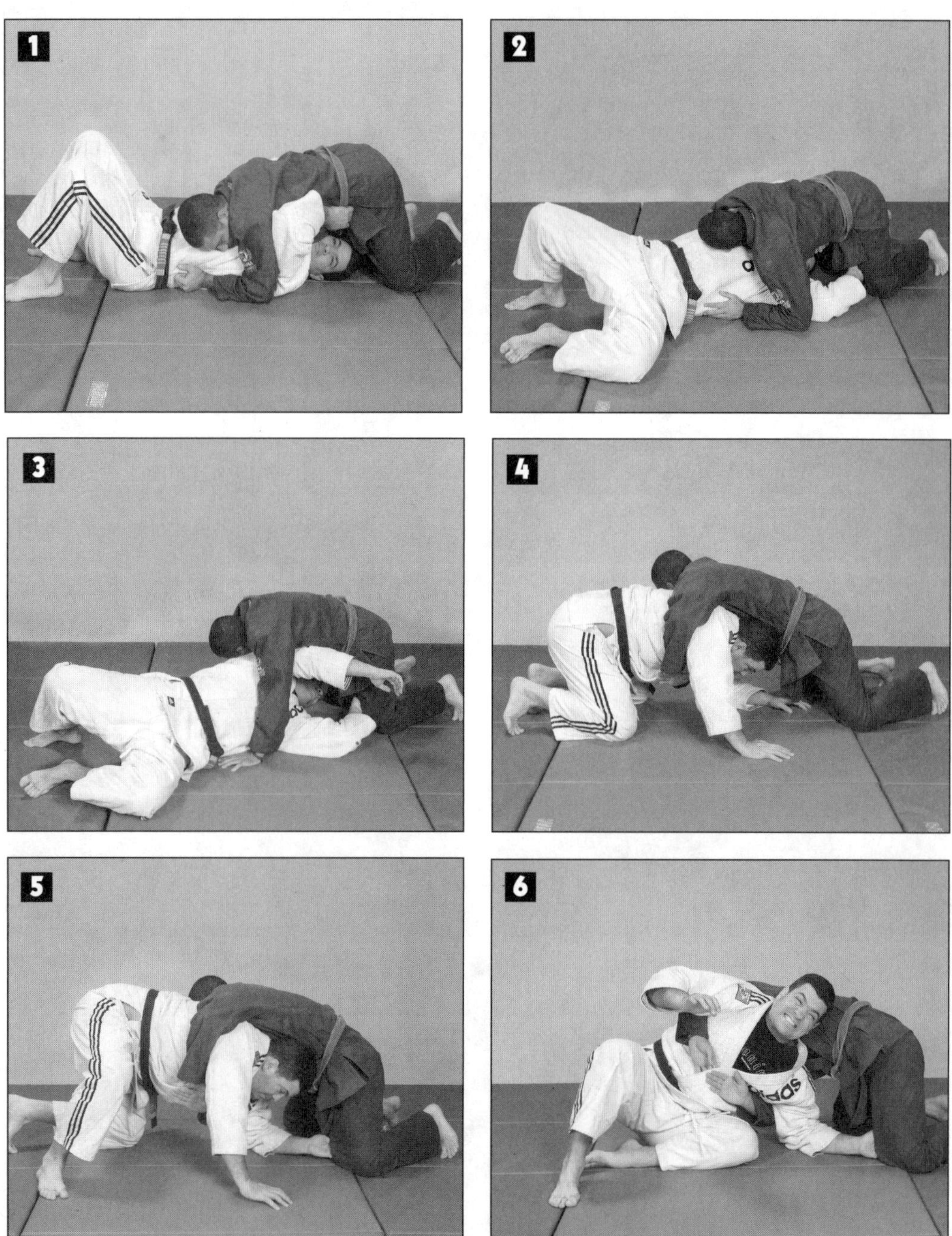
1
2
3
4
5
6

North & South 8

7

8

9

The fighters are in the north-south position, and Rigan is under the opponent (1). As he grabs the opponent's left leg, Rigan slides away (2). Using his left hand to support himself, Rigan starts turning to the side (3) until he is on his hands and knees (4). He grabs the adversary's left leg, shifts to the right (5), raises his head (6) and escapes (7). He immediately seizes the opportunity to turn (8) and mount the opponent from behind (9).

1
2
3
4
5
6

North & South 9

The combatants begin in the north-south position, and Rigan is on the bottom (1). Rigan grabs the opponent's left leg and slides away (2). Using his left hand for support, Rigan flips over until he is on his hands and knees (3). Utilizing his right arm, Rigan grabs the opponent's left arm (4). Rigan raises his body (5), turns to the right (6-7) and throws his opponent (8). After assuming side control, Rigan initiates the offense (9).

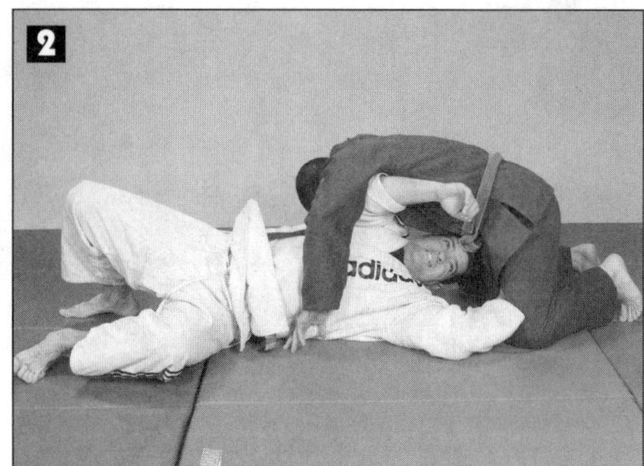

Rigan is on the bottom as the pair begins in the north-south position (1). Rigan grabs the opponent's left leg, pushes himself away (2), twists and gets on his hands and knees (3). Rigan sits in front of the opponent (4), places his left foot inside the opponent's legs (5)

and sweeps him to the side (6). Rigan rolls with him (7) and assumes side control so he can initiate the attack (8).

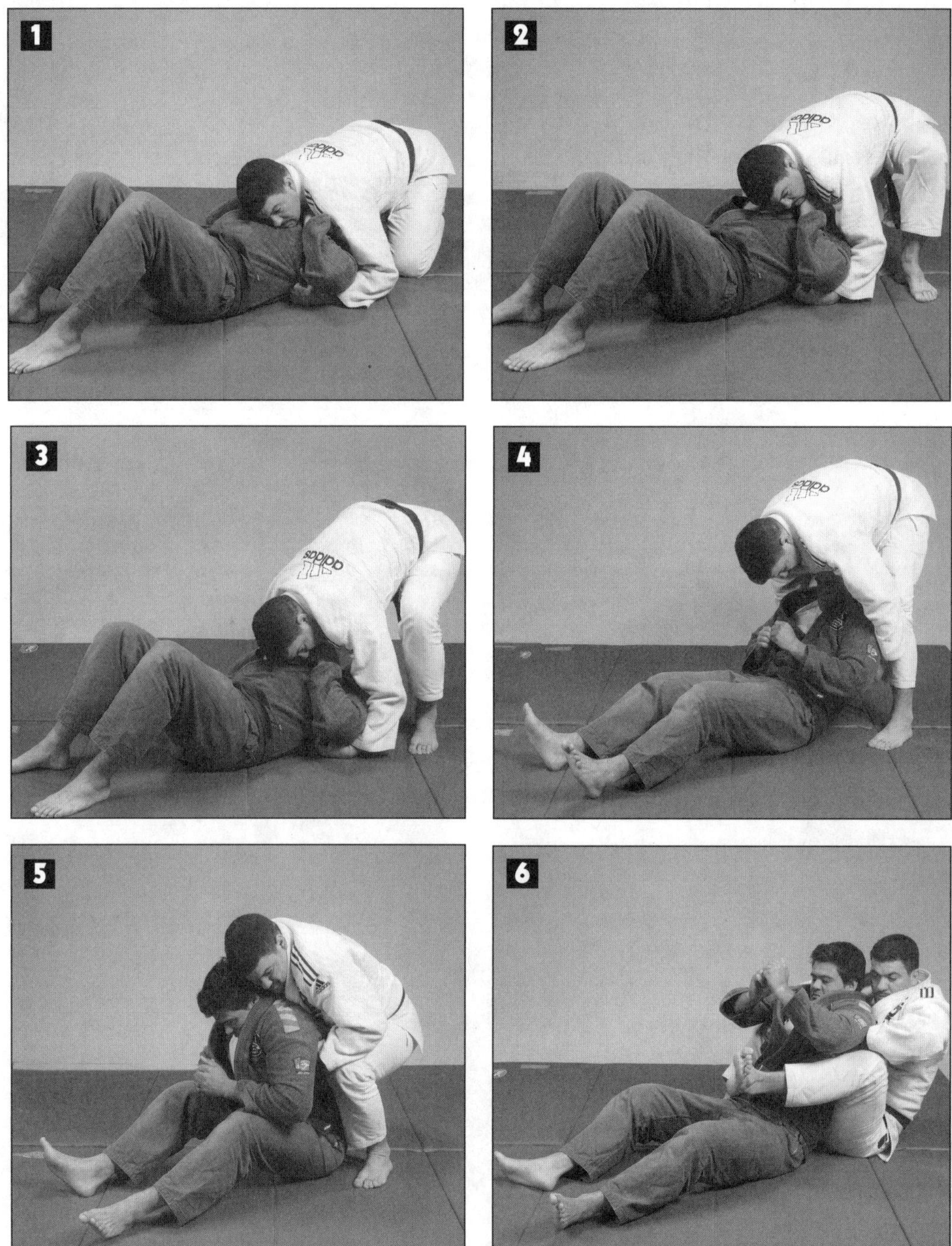
1
2
3
4
5
6

North & South 11

7

8

9

While in the north-south position, Rigan controls the opponent (1). Rigan moves backwards, gets on his feet and grabs both of the opponent's armpits (2). He stands (3), pulls the opponent upright (4) and quickly starts to sit (5). Once Rigan is on the ground (6), he quickly "hooks" the opponent (7). Note the position of his feet. Employing his right hand, Rigan opens the opponent's collar (8). He uses his left hand to grab the lapel, and he cranks on the choke (9).

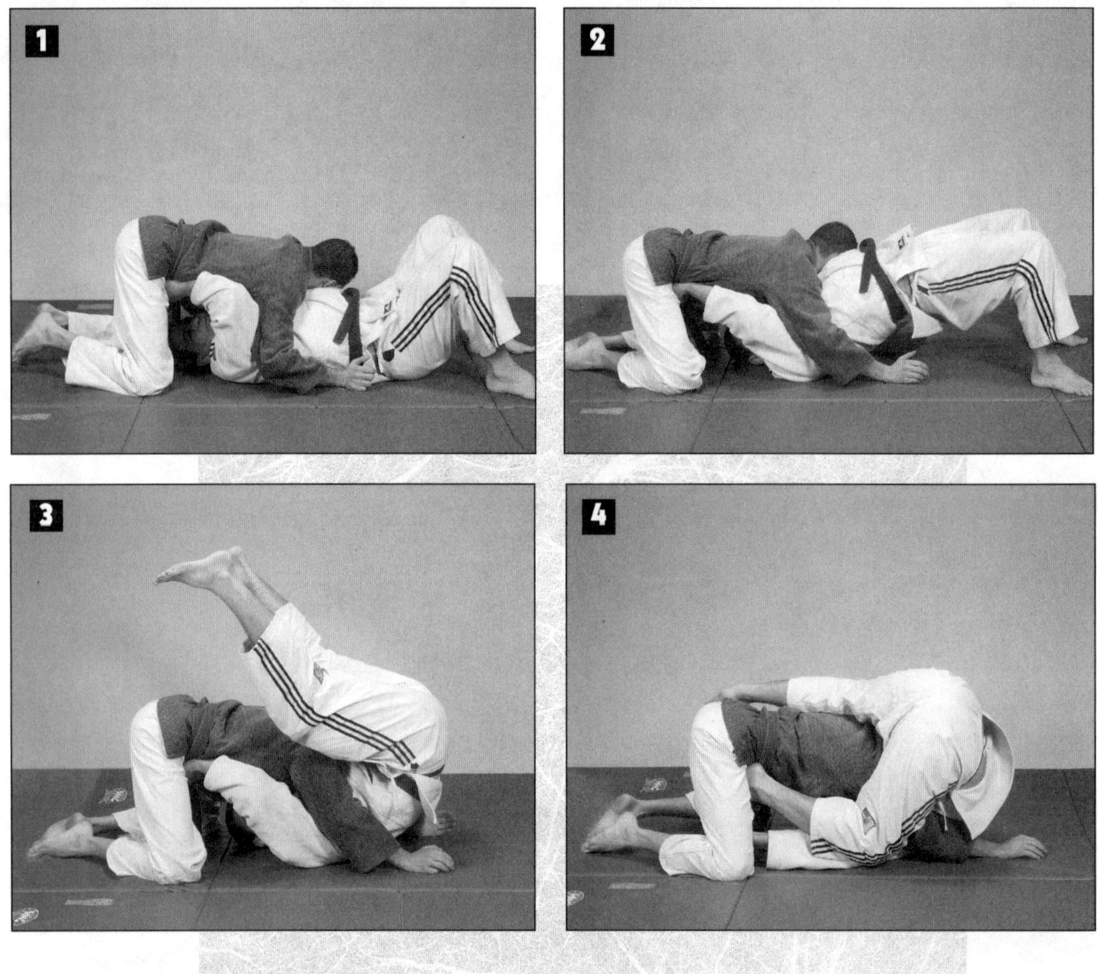

Rigan is under his opponent in the north-south position (1). To avoid the pressure, Rigan pushes the opponent's hips with both hands and slides his hips forward (2). He raises his legs (3) and escapes from the bottom (4).

North & South 12

He scrambles to the opponent's back (5) and gets ready to initiate the attack (6).

Breaking The Grip

Vol. 3

The opponent prevents Rigan from getting an armlock by grabbing his own wrist (1). With his left arm under the opponent's arms (2), Rigan slides his right arm under and grabs the opponent's left hand (3),

Breaking The Grip 1

twists to the side and simultaneously pulls back. This creates a wristlock that allows him to break the opponent's grip (4). He leans back, pulls the arm and executes the final armlock (5).

Utilizing the "fingers-with-fingers" grip, the opponent prevents Rigan from getting an armlock (1). As Rigan grabs his own gi to secure the grip, he moves his left foot onto the opponent's right arm (2). As he pushes the arm with his foot, he releases his gi, grabs the opponent's hands and pulls (3).

Breaking The Grip 2

He breaks the grip (4), leans back and applies the straight armlock (5).

By grabbing his own forearms, the opponent prevents Rigan from getting an armlock (1). Rigan places his left leg inside the opponent's arms as he secures both arms with his right hand (2). Then he pulls the opponent closer (3),

Breaking The Grip 3

leans back, guides the opponent's head closer (4) and executes a *triangle* choke (5).

To prevent Rigan from getting an armlock, the opponent grabs his own arms (1). Rigan places his left leg on top of the opponent's arms (2) and hooks his left foot under his right leg to apply pressure (3).

Breaking The Grip 4

As he pulls back with his hands, he pushes down with his legs, breaking the grip (4). He now executes an armlock (5).

The opponent prevents the armlock by grabbing Rigan's legs (1). Using his right hand, Rigan grabs the opponent's right arm (2). He then leans forward (3) and mounts his opponent as he maintains control of both arms (4).

Breaking The Grip 5

Rigan quickly switches positions (5), swings his left leg over, leans back and applies a straight armlock to the opposite arm (6). Note: Keep total control of both arms while you are moving from side to side. If you lose the grip, you will lose control.

To prevent the armlock, the opponent grabs his lapel (1). To create some maneuvering room, Rigan slightly moves his hips (2). Employing his right hand, Rigan grabs the opponent's collar (3), pushes forward (4)

Breaking The Grip 6

and breaks the grip (5). Now he can execute the final armlock (6).

To prevent Rigan from getting an armlock, the opponent grabs his own forearms (1). Rigan clutches his hands together (2). Note that his left arm is between the opponent's arms. He pulls back (3),

Breaking The Grip 7

and keeps leaning until he breaks the grip (4). He can now apply an armlock (5).

The opponent prevents Rigan from getting an armlock by grabbing his own triceps (1). Rigan places both hands on the opponent's right triceps (2) and pulls hard. This creates pressure in the wrists, which eventually will break the grip (3). To assist in this maneuver, notice how he uses his left leg to generate additional pressure (4).

Breaking The Grip 8

5

He hooks his left foot under his right leg (5) and easily applies a reverse straight armlock (6).

6

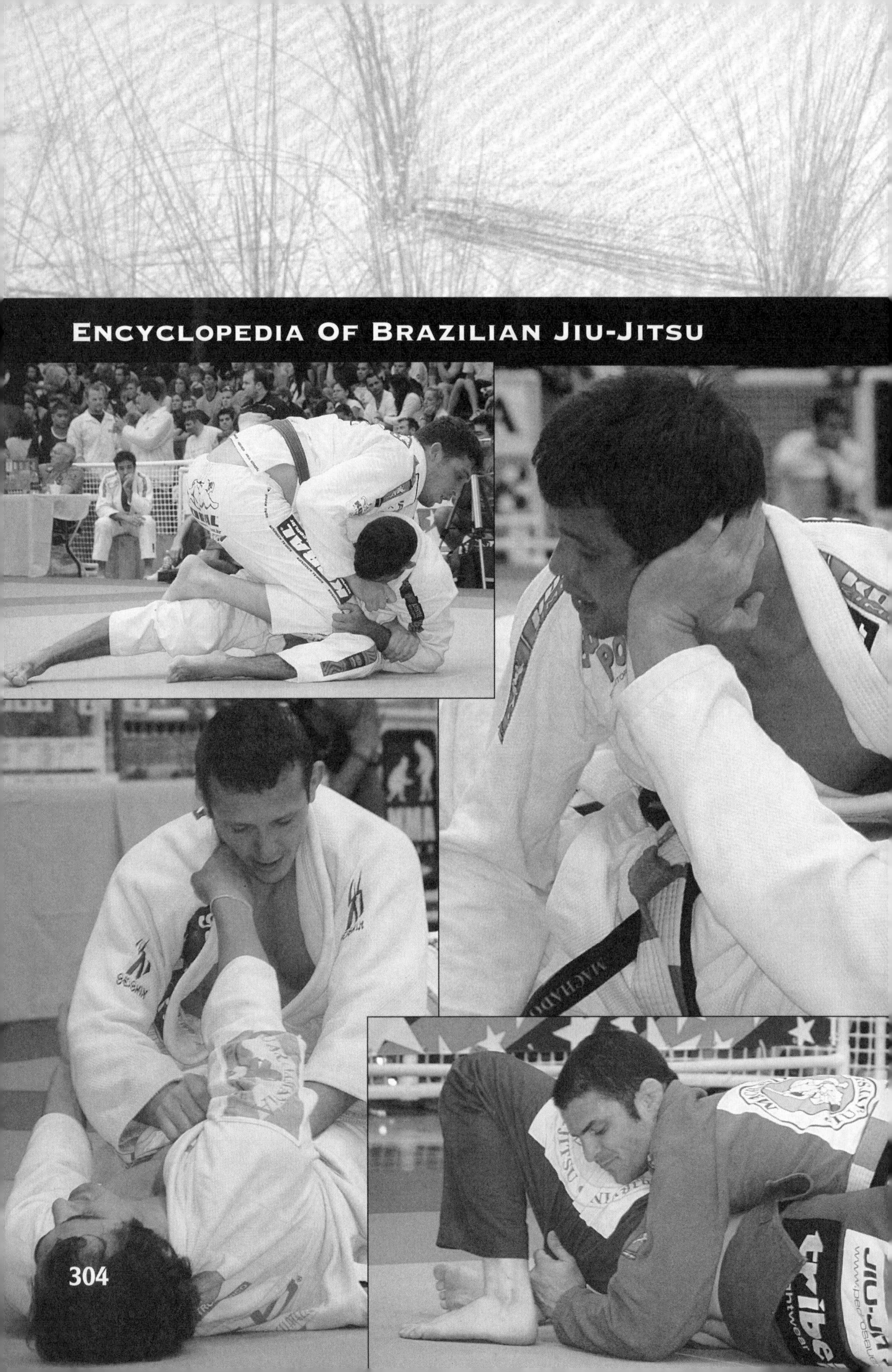

Rules
Part 3

Vol. 3

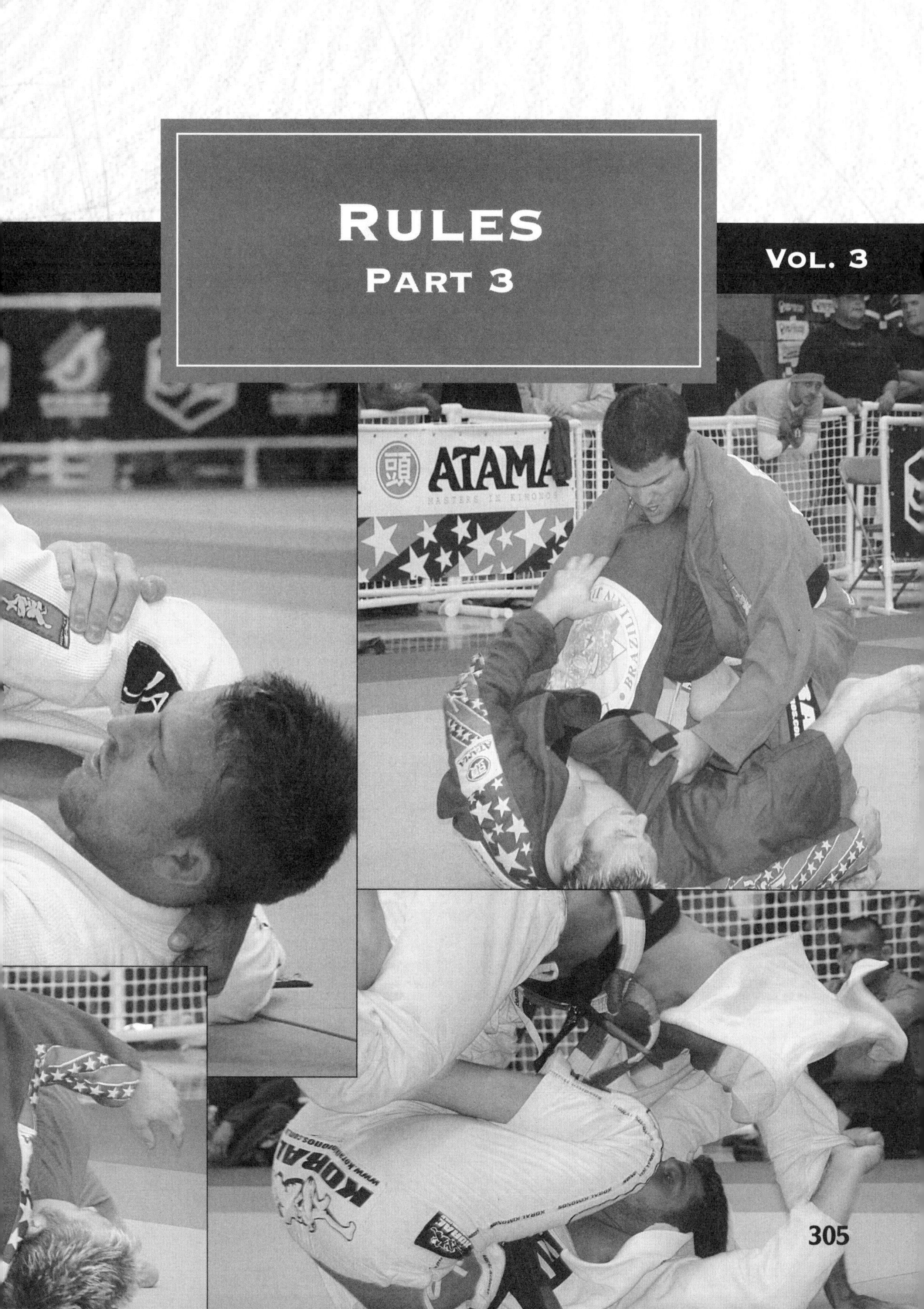

Rules

International Brazilian Jiu-Jitsu Federation
Technical Department of Regulations and Rules
Part 3

Article No. 6: Restrictions

- When a competitor is in danger of serious bodily harm as a result of a submission, the central referee has the authority to stop a match and award the victory to the competitor applying the submission.
- Cervical locks or neck cranks are not allowed under any circumstances, and there are no exceptions. Competitors attempting a cervical lock will be immediately disqualified, even if they have not had any prior warnings.

- Athletes younger than 18 (juveniles) are only allowed to compete in the open class if they are middleweight or heavier.
- Wrestling shoes or any other type of shoes, headgear, shirts under the gi and any kind of protectors that can alter the outcome of the match in any way are prohibited.
- When a competitor between the age of 4 and 15 is executing a triangle and the opponent stands, it is the referee's obligation to stand in a position to protect both athletes, specifically to reduce the risk of cervical damage.

The following techniques are prohibited for competitors between the ages of 4 through 12:

- Knee lock, leg lock
- Cervical lock of any kind
- Frontal mata-leao
- Bate estaca
- Biceps lock
- Mao de vaca
- Triangle pulling the head
- Foot locks of any kind
- Ezequiel
- Calf lock
- Omoplata (shoulder lock)
- Technical frontal tie (guillotine)
- Kami-basami (scissor take down)
- Heel hook

The following techniques are prohibited for competitors between the ages of 13 through 15:

- Bate estaca
- Biceps lock
- Mao de vaca
- Triangle (pulling the head)
- Foot locks of any kind
- Knee lock or leg lock
- Cervical lock of any kind
- Frontal mata-leao
- Ezequiel
- Calf lock
- Kami-basami (scissor take down)
- Heel hook

The following techniques are prohibited for competitors between the ages of 16 to 17:

- Bate estaca
- Leg locks
- Cervical techniques
- Biceps lock
- Calf lock
- Mao de vaca
- Mata-leao with foot
- Kami-basami (scissor take down)
- Heel hook

The following techniques are prohibited for adult through senior competitors (blue & purple belt):

- Mata-leao with foot
- Bate estaca
- Leg locks
- Cervical techniques
- Biceps locks
- Calf locks
- Kami-basami (scissor take down)
- Heel hooks

The following techniques are prohibited for adult through senior competitors (brown & black belt):

- Biceps locks
- Cervical locks
- Kami-basami (scissor take down)
- Heel hooks

Article No. 7: Hygiene

a) The kimono must be washed and dried and have no unpleasant odors.

b) Toe and fingernails must be cut short and be clean.

c) During the match, competitors must keep their hair from interfering with their opponents or themselves.

d) "Painting" or using hair gels to temporarily color your hair is prohibited and may result in disqualification.

Article No. 8: Kimono

To compete, competitors must abide by the hygiene and kimono specifications that follow.

a) The uniform must be constructed of cotton or similar material and be in good condition. The material may not be excessively thick or so hard that it will obstruct the opponent in any way.

b) The uniform may be white or blue, but it's improper to combine colors, such as a white jacket and blue pants.

c) The jacket should reach the competitor's thighs, and the sleeves must reach the wrist with the arms extended in front of the body.

d) The belt should be 4-5 cm wide, the color should correspond to the fighter's rank and the belt should be tied around the competitor's waist tight enough to secure the kimono so that it is closed.

e) Athletes are not permitted to compete with torn kimonos or with sleeves that are not of the proper length. Only females are permitted to wear t-shirts underneath the kimono.

Article No. 9: Fight Durations

In the championship bouts, following are the length of the fights:

- Pre-pee-wee — 2 minutes
- Pee-wee — 3 minutes
- Infants — 4 minutes
- Infants/Juvenile — 4 minutes
- Juvenile — 5 minutes

A) ADULT

- White belt — 5 minutes
- Blue belt — 6 minutes
- Purple — 7 minutes
- Brown — 8 minutes
- Black — 10 minutes

B) MASTER

- Blue — 5 minutes
- Purple — 6 minutes
- Brown — 6 minutes
- Black — 6 minutes

C) SENIOR

- Blue — 5 minutes
- Purple — 5 minutes
- Brown — 5 minutes
- Black — 5 minutes

D) The times for the 5x5 championships are as follows:

Men

- Blue — 6 minutes
- Purple — 6 minutes
- Brown and black — 10 minutes

Women

- Blue — 6 minutes
- Purple, brown and black — 7 minutes

Article No. 10: Direction and Decision

1. During a competition, technicians, professors, directors, timekeepers and selected other officials all serve in an official capacity. Anyone else is prohibited from giving instructions to the competitor from inside the competition area. If this happens, the competitor can be disqualified.

2. If both athletes are injured and unable to continue during the final match, the result will be determined by the scorecard.

A. If points or advantages are confirmed, they will determine the winner.

B. If no points or advantages exist, the result will be a draw.

3. If the two athletes stand from a position on the ground in any situation, the judgment will be equal to that if standing.

4. For the final matches, there will be a maximum of twice as many rest periods for the athletes.

5. For the final match, the competitors will be allowed two opportunities to make weight.

6. If one of the competitors does not show for the final match, the athlete present will be awarded the win and the other competitor will not receive a medal.

Epilogue

Now that you have finished this book, what have you learned? Hopefully nothing less than a series of practical and efficient techniques for becoming a successful Brazilian Jiu-Jitsu practitioner. These methods and training practices will help you succeed in competition and also to learn and grow after each defeat. These techniques have been developed by world-class competitors who have successfully applied them in elite competition. By using these same methods, you can also enjoy success in your own matches, even if you're not a world-class competitor. But simply reading through these pages is not enough. You must consistently practice each technique with a training partner, exploring all the possibilities of each position, until you obtain the desired results based on your body style, athletic ability, and physical attributes. Not all positions and techniques will work for every practitioner. Once you have a basic framework in place, you must fine-tune each position until it fits your game. The enjoyable part of Brazilian Jiu-Jitsu is that everyone can adapt and personalize it. While the basics are the same, the application of the basics is as different and varied as each practitioner. When practiced under the guidance of a qualified instructor, or with the assistance of a willing training partner, the principles and methods explained in these volumes will be effective. This is because they have been tested and proven for decades in the laboratory of practical experience and the crucible of real competition. Your task now is simply to go out and have fun with them!

— The authors